"...And they loved not their lives unto the death."

THE CRUCIFIED ONES

CALLING FORTH
THE END-TIME REMNANT

by

Charles Elliott Newbold, Jr.

Ingathering Press

Published by Ingathering Press

For ordering additional copies of this book or for information on other books this author has published, write or call:
Ingathering Press
306 Cumberland Cove Road
Monterey, Tennessee 38574
1-931-839-8078

Unless otherwise marked, scripture quotations are taken from the King James Version of the Bible, with certain words changed to their modern equivalent; for example, "thou" has been changed to "you," and "saith" has been changed to "says."

Scriptures marked NAS are taken from the New American Standard Bible, © The Lockman Foundation 1960, 1962, 1963, 1968, 1971, 1972, 1973, 1975, 1977.

Scriptures marked NKJV are taken from The Holy Bible, New King James Version. Copyright © 1982, 1983 by Thomas Nelson, Inc.

ISBN 0-9647766-0-X

Printed in the United States of America

Contents

Introduction

Shortly after the first of the year of 1990, I began to write under inspiration the following chapters which, to my satisfaction, help explain the new thing God is doing today: namely, He is bringing forth a new order of Christians who are of the John the Baptist (Elijah) anointing, preparing the way of the Lord—the end-time remnant.

They are forerunners to the fulfillment of the Feast of Tabernacles. I call this new order of Christians "the crucified ones." I do not capitalize their name for to do so would violate their very nature and purpose in the world today. This study is given to identifying these crucified ones.

To best understand this new order of Christians is to see them in terms of how God Himself foreshadowed spiritual events in the three main feasts of Israel's worship as they correspond to the three courts of the Tabernacle of Moses.

This is not intended to be an extensive study on the feasts and courts themselves. There are many scholars far more qualified to teach on them than I. Many men of revelation have long before seen how these things foreshadowed all that Christ fulfilled in the New Testament. Only enough is given here to see specifically how they relate to the upward call of God in Christ Jesus in these crucified ones.

It certainly is my prayer that as you study this book, it will serve to call you forth into sonship, into a walk of total obedience—that it will utterly change your life.

Further, this reading should help you come to a better understanding of the great works of Christ identified in such words as justification, redemption, sanctification,

1

and glorification, and how they relate to one another as the progressive work of salvation in God's eternal purposes.

As you read, always pray for the Holy Spirit to teach you and to give you a spirit of wisdom and discernment. Moreover, ask Him to take hold of your life in such a way as to bring you into fullness in Him.

Chapter 1

Three Feasts and Three Courts

Why did God ordain that Israel should celebrate the three main feasts of Passover, Pentecost, and Tabernacles? And why are there three courts in the Tabernacle of Moses in the wilderness as well as in Solomon's Temple? Are these simply capricious thoughts on the part of God? Certainly God had a plan in mind. Certainly He has a purpose for these. These were a pattern for something to come.

The feasts, the three courts, all of the furnishings and utensils in the Tabernacle and Temple, the rituals—I believe that all of these speak of things unique in His Kingdom that were fulfilled one way or the other in Jesus Christ. First, He was Savior in fulfillment of Passover. Then, He was Sanctifier in the gift of His Holy Spirit in the fulfillment of Pentecost. Finally, He will come again as Glorifier in His glorified body with His glorified holy ones at His side in the fulfillment of Tabernacles.

The Old Testament symbols are rich in what they reveal to us today. Thank God as we approach that great and terrible day of the Lord that these truths are being revealed to the church and are calling us onward and upward into Him as He prepares His bride for His coming. The preparation of the bride is the preparation for His coming. They work together.

These three feasts and courts also reveal where different members of the body of Christ are in terms of their relationship with Him. It is important that we understand that we can have varying degrees of relationship with Him—not that He would have it that way, but that we, nevertheless, in our stubborn and willful ways, have it that

3

way. This chapter explores how I see these differences in our relationship to Christ.

Categories of Believers

While there are many denominations and variations of groups in Christianity, I basically see five categories of believers that spread across all of these groups. They are liberals, evangelicals, Pentecostals, charismatics, and an emerging group I will call, for the want of a better term, the "crucified ones."

For the most part, liberals, evangelicals, Pentecostals, and charismatics remain a part of institutional Christianity. While most denominations tend to fit into one of these categories, we often find a mix of individuals holding to these different persuasions within them all. These individuals differ from one another in terms of their doctrines which inclines them toward different interests.

The following description is simplistic and general. Space or purpose does not permit fuller explanation.

Liberals have generally believed in a social gospel and have been inclined toward humanism and social reform.

Evangelicals have preached the blood atonement of Jesus Christ, the necessity of the rebirth experience, and have been inclined toward fundamentalism.

Both Pentecostals and charismatics have had in common the belief in the baptism in the Holy Spirit, speaking in unknown tongues, and in various other gifts of the Spirit. Otherwise, there has been a vast difference between these two groups.

Pentecostals have preached holiness which, for them, was attained through systems of religious codes designed to control the outward behavior of their constituents. They have been, therefore, inclined toward legalism.

Charismatics (especially among those in "Word" churches) have preached faith and prosperity which has inclined them toward self-ism and materialism.

The "crucified ones" preach Christ and Him crucified and are inclined toward absolute obedience to the Holy Spirit at all cost to self. The rest of this study is given to the identification of these crucified ones.

I believe these differing groups are typified in the three main Old Testament feasts of the Jewish sacred year as well as in the three courts of the Tabernacle of Moses. These feasts and courts correlate with several other features having to do with our pressing onward in the high calling of God.

Chart

The following chart of these correlations is adapted from a teaching which I first heard from the late Bro. Bill Britton, a prophet of God from Springfield, Missouri. The Lord has made this correlation real to me over the years and has added some understanding of it to me. Other teachers also have confirming correlations. The following parallels somewhat guide the outline within this study and will be further explained in later chapters.

Read across the columns, left to right.

1st	2nd	3rd
Passover	Pentecost	Tabernacles
Death, Burial, Resurrection, & Ascension	Outpouring of Holy Spirit	Second Coming of Christ
Outer Court	Holy Place	Holy of Holies
Evangelicals	Pentecostals/ Charismatics	"crucified ones"
Jesus-Savior	Christ-Anointed	Lord-King
Thirtyfold	Sixtyfold	Hundredfold
Traditional	"Spirit Filled"	Spirit Led
Justification	Sanctification	Glorification
Consume Christ/ Consumed by Him	Consumed with Christ	Consuming Fire for Christ
Spirit Redeemed	Soul Being Renewed	Body to Be Glorified
Water Baptism	Holy Spirit Baptism	Baptism of Sufferings
Children	Sons	Fathers
Way	Truth	Life
See the Kingdom	Enter the Kingdom	Inherit the Kingdom
Israel (Samaria)	Judah	Zion

If you are not already familiar with the Old Testament feasts and the design of the Tabernacle, it would be best to read Leviticus 23 and Exodus 25-27 before going on.

The outer court of Moses' Tabernacle where the animal sacrifices were made corresponds with the Feast of Passover which was fulfilled in the death, burial, resurrection, and ascension of Jesus Christ.

The Holy Place with the altar of incense, the table of showbread (the bread of preparation), and the candlesticks, which continually burned olive oil, corresponds with the Feast of Pentecost which was fulfilled in the outpouring of the Holy Spirit upon the church on the day of Pentecost (Acts 2).

The Holy of Holies, wherein is the ark of the covenant with the mercy seat on it, corresponds with the Feast of Tabernacles (also called Feast of Booths) which has yet to be completely fulfilled. Once a year, on the Day of Atonement, the high priest entered behind the veil into the Holy of Holies to sprinkle the blood of animal sacrifices upon the mercy seat to atone for his own sins and for the sins of the people (Ex. 30:10). Jesus partially fulfilled the day of Atonement as our great High Priest (Heb. 9:7-12).

Tabernacles is also known as the Feast of Ingathering (Ex. 23:16) which I believe represents that great ingathering into Jesus on that great and terrible day of the Lord when He comes again.

I find that the various groups of Christians fit into one or the other of these different courts or feasts, depending on their willingness to go further in Jesus Christ as Lord. It is as though some have entered into the Kingdom of God but have not yet inherited all that is theirs to be enjoyed.

I don't mean to be ugly in doing so, but I place the liberals outside of the Tabernacle walls altogether and dispense with further discussion about them since most of them reject the divine inspiration of scripture. Consequently, they deny most of the fundamental truths of the Christian faith. I leave the matter of their salvation up to God. (I applaud their humanitarian interests and could wish the whole church were more taken up with these works. But our interest here has to do with relationship with God and not with works.)

I place the evangelicals in the outer court of the Tabernacle since they believe in the blood atonement of the Lamb of God and in the rebirth experience which is clearly represented in the Feast of Passover. But, by their own confession, that's as far as they go. For the most part they are able only to bear fruit thirtyfold, lacking the power of the Holy Spirit. Claiming to have the baptism in the Holy Spirit on the basis of doctrine doesn't get it.

The Pentecostals and charismatics believe in the blood atonement, rebirth experience, and go one step further. They believe in and have received the baptism in the Holy Spirit (empowering) as promised by the Father which is typified in the Holy Place of the Tabernacle. But this is as far as they go. As a rule, they too have camped out around their "Pentecostal" experiences. They fail to recognize that the Holy Spirit was given to empower them to go on into the Holy of Holies; that is, into a place of absolute Lordship of Jesus Christ. While most would confess, as would the evangelicals, that Jesus Christ is Lord, the reality of that is not in their walk but only in their talk.

The Pentecostals and charismatics, having received the power of the Holy Spirit, have the potential of bearing fruit sixtyfold. Too often, however, they have viewed the Pentecostal experience as an end rather than the means toward the end: total surrender to the Lordship of Jesus Christ.

The new breed of radical believers, the "crucified ones," not only believe in the blood atonement, the new birth, and the Pentecostal experience, but are pressing into the Holy of Holies where the Feast of Tabernacles is to be fulfilled. The Holy of Holies is the place in the Spirit where nothing else matters but Jesus Christ and His absolute will. They are learning the full implication of what it means to lay one's life down for the sake of the gospel.

While Tabernacles is yet to be fulfilled, there are forerunners to it. Just as John the Baptist was a forerunner to prepare the way of the Lord, so are these crucified ones forerunners to prepare the way of the Lord's second coming. Previously, John was one man with the anointing of the Elijah spirit (Luke 1:17). These last-days forerunners are a many-membered man with the Elijah spirit—prophets by nature and lifestyle!

Traditional, "Spirit-filled," and Spirit-led Believers

There is another way to make these distinctions: there are the traditional churches, so-called "Spirit-filled" churches, and the Spirit-led believers.

I say so-called "Spirit-filled" churches because these are they who started out being led by the Spirit but somewhere along the way camped out around their past experiences, institutionalized them, and have gone no further. When you cease to be "Spirit-led," you soon become traditional again. So in the long run, there are only two divisions: traditionalist and Spirit-led. All traditionalists end up becoming another sect within institutional Christianity while the Spirit-led rarely find affinity with an organized group.

We notice that the world accepts the traditional church, it tolerates the Spirit-filled church, but it will crucify the Spirit-led believers. Even the traditionalists in Christianity regard the Spirit-led believers with disdain.

If Satan and the powers of darkness could ever stop the people of God from being led by the Spirit of God, they would successfully thwart the power of God because the power of God is released through obedience. The enemy is never threatened by those *"having a form of godliness, but denying the power thereof..."* (2 Tim. 3:5).

The enemy is threatened, however, by a company of overcomers today who dare to deny themselves and take up their cross daily (Luke 9:23), who dare to follow the Lamb wherever He goes. He trembles at the very emergence of these crucified ones.

Chapter 2

Going Through the Cross

I call this third group of believers the "crucified ones" because I see them as having not only gone to the cross for the forgiveness of their sins, but as having gone through the cross in total denial of anything for self. Each is willing, as Jesus called, to *"take up his cross daily..."* (Luke 9:23, Matt. 16:24).

These crucified ones are dead so far as the interests and deeds of their flesh and of the world are concerned. They have come to the end of themselves—the place God wants to bring us all. They understand that the only true life is found in the loss of their own self-life, to be given over completely to the absolute will of God. *"Whoever will save his life shall lose it"* (Matt. 16:25). They are willing to die, or willing to be made willing to die, for the sake of the gospel.

Jesus is the only issue in their lives. Other great truths and doctrines are important as safeguards against heresy, but, to them, these truths never become dividing issues in the body of Christ. These "crucified ones" are not argumentative or divisive but are, nonetheless, bulwarks for the Truth who is Jesus Christ as Lord.

Under the Headship/Lordship of Christ

The crucified ones have a strong sense of and security in the headship of Jesus Christ. They resist the pressures of traditional Christianity to submit to the headship of other men but are given to the scriptural order of 1 Corinthians 11: 3: *"But I would have you know, that the head of every man is Christ; and the head of the woman is the man; and the head of Christ is God."* Any other headship, to them, would be false and offensive to their sincere spirits.

Their insistence upon the headship of Jesus Christ is an offense to the traditionalists/institutionalists who, for some reason, want to bring men into submission to men.

Nevertheless, the crucified ones are submitted one to another, especially to those others who are sensitive to the leadings of the Holy Spirit. Having come through the cross as it were, they are humble, broken before the Lord, and eager to examine themselves to see if there is any evil within. They voluntarily and willfully present themselves accountable one to another.

They have no ambition for self but see themselves as servants. They are willing to do their service before God in secret, making no acclaim for themselves. They do not seek for themselves *"a city, and a tower, ...and a name"* (Gen. 11:4). They are without ambition to increase themselves in power, position, or riches. They are not interested in building churches and memberships for themselves, devising programs, or gaining reputation and titles. They have no agenda of their own. They only want and pursue what God wants.

While they are genuinely submitted one to the other in the Spirit, they are not motivated by the fear of man but by their reverence for God Almighty. Jesus is absolute Lord in their lives. They have renounced all forms of idolatry.

Radical Obedience

The absolute Lordship of Jesus Christ infers radical obedience to Him. The crucified ones have abandoned all to follow Him and are faithful in the least as well as in the greater of things (Luke 16:10).

Such obedience comes out of extreme faith and confidence in God as being sovereign in their lives. Their faith supersedes faith for things, even the things of the Kingdom. Their faith is in God regardless of things and circumstances.

Yet, they are not without knowledge of the wiles of the devil nor without power over all the work of the enemy. In fact, they exert absolute power over the enemy because they are obedient to the Spirit.

They have such confidence in the greater power of God in them that whatever happens to them is regarded more as the sanctification work of the Holy Spirit than as the destructive work of the enemy. They are so given to God and His will that they have that confidence that *"...all things work together for good to them that love God, to them who are the called according to His purpose"* (Rom. 8:28).

Non-Religious

The crucified ones are non-religious non-traditional, non-institutional, and non-liturgical. They see the difference between religion and relationship. They do not need religion because they have a personal relationship with the Christ of Christianity.

Religion is interested in the doing of things to appease the gods while relationship is interested in being in fellowship with the God-person Himself.

Religion is sacrifice; relationship is obedience. Religion is intent on cleaning the outside of the cup; relationship is intent upon being cleansed on the inside (Matt. 23:25-26).

Religion partakes of the symbol only of the body and the blood (communion); relationship partakes of the Person of the body and the blood.

We can no longer offer people the symbol only. They need the Person of the symbol—Jesus Christ, Lord

The crucified ones no longer base their own lives on the symbol but upon their relationship with the Person. They are so identified with Him that, when they present their own lives as a living sacrifice holy and acceptable unto God (Rom. 12:1), it is as though they are presenting the Person Himself.

Being in relationship with God this way, they will come to know Him, not just know about Him—to understand Him and His ways, to trust Him, to have love and affection for Him, to fear Him, to respect Him, and to obey Him. An inseparable bond is formed between Him and them.

The interest of these crucified ones is to seek only more and more of Jesus. They are those for whom it could be said by their life and power *"that they had been with Jesus"* (Acts 4:13).

They are not centered upon themselves in any way but are centered and focused upon Jesus and His will. They identify with His plans and purposes in all eternity.

Non-materialistic

They are non-materialistic, having learned that *"a man's life does not consist in the abundance of the things which he possesses"* (Luke 12:15). They identify with the apostle Paul who said of himself, *"...I have learned, in whatsoever state I am, therewith to be content"* (Phil. 4:11). It does not matter whether they have or have not. Their confidence is in their God who provides. They think Spirit, not flesh; eternal, not temporal; spiritual, not material.

Non-Sensational

They are non-sensational. They are Spirit-immersed, likely to speak in unknown tongues, believe in the present day operation of the gifts and ministries of the Spirit as set forth in the scriptures, and are anxiously awaiting the second coming of the Lord. But these things are no longer the issue with them. Their interest is to receive spiritual gifts as tools to go on in the Lordship of Jesus Christ.

The Pentecostal experience is not the end, but the means toward the higher goal of attaining Him, of being found in Him (Phil. 3: 7-11). They are less inclined to seek the sensational, outward manifestations of miracles and healings and more inclined to seek that *"holiness without which no man shall see the Lord"* (Heb. 12:14). They desire more that hidden work of the Holy Spirit in their lives. In the long run, however, the greater and truer signs will follow them.

Their main interest is to be separated unto God. *"For this is the will of God, even your sanctification..."* (1 Thess. 4:3). They are quick to admit to sin and to repent.

Holiness, to them, is attained through the purging, purifying, cleansing fire of the Holy Spirit—transforming and conforming them into the image of Jesus.

They are patient to wait upon the Lord—to rest, wait, listen, and then and only then, to do.

They have a profound confidence in the Bible as the word of God and live as though God said what He meant and meant what He said.

They also have a profound confidence in the Holy Spirit of God and operate on the basis of Zechariah 4:6: *"Not by might, nor by power but by My Spirit, says the Lord of hosts."* They put no confidence in the flesh (Phil. 3:3).

The Church without Walls

The crucified ones are the church without walls. They have gone outside of the camp with Jesus, bearing His reproach (Heb. 13:12-13).

The churches are like walled cities within which to keep their own.

The ecumenical movement is an attempt to overlap these walls so as to give an appearance of unity. But all of these attempts will never remove the reality of the walls.

More often, even among the most sincere believers, these walled cities become social clubs for their kind. God is not calling for Christian country clubs. Rather He is calling for His people to come out of them. The only wall that God and His crucified ones are interested in is that wall of fire mentioned in Zechariah 2:5: *"'For I,' says the Lord, 'will be unto her a wall of fire round about, and will be the glory in the midst of her.'"* These crucified ones are a people who have been called out of a people: the *ekklesia*, "called out ones."*

They view the gifts of the Spirit and the ministries of the Spirit as belonging to the whole body without regard to particular church membership.

The crucified ones have taken for themselves no other name but His name: the name of Jesus (Acts 15:14).

---

*Ekklesia is the Greek word that has been translated "church" but which literally means "called-out ones."

13

They gather in no other name but His (Matt. 18:20).

They submit to no other headship/Lordship except the headship/Lordship of Jesus Christ who is the true head of the church (Eph. 1:22; 4:15; 5:23).

They follow no one but the Holy Spirit of God who is Himself bound only to do and say what Jesus, the Head, is doing and saying (John 16:13).

They know no other voice but that of the Good Shepherd (John 10:14-16).

They are joined to no one or no thing but to Him (1 Cor. 6:17).

They have been bought with a price (1 Cor. 7:23) and, therefore, dare not attempt to own anyone or to be owned by anyone except Him. Yet, they belong to each other in the deepest spiritual sense of the word (1 Cor. 3:22 NAS).

They have no other life to live but that His life should be lived in and through them (Gal. 2:20).

Prophets

The crucified ones are a people who say what God says, do what God does, and are what God has made them to be.

They are true prophets of God. By the use of the term prophet, I do not infer that they are all called to the equipping gift ministry of prophet. Nevertheless, their lives are styled after that of the prophets of God—the Elijah spirit—having this radical relationship with God in the Spirit, speaking for God by their very life-style, bringing conviction to the world, preparing the way of the Lord's second coming.

They appear as mavericks in the body of Christ but are in fact the very opposite. They are each given absolutely to the will of God at all cost to themselves. There is no rebellion to be found within them.

As each of them follow the Spirit, they find that He leads according to the Scriptures; that the gifts and ministries of the Spirit will emerge and begin to flow together without walls; that His body, the church, will begin to come together in good scriptural order and liberty as one man according to Ephesians 4:13; that His divine purposes and plans are revealed; that His presence and power is manifested; and that they themselves are emerging as a corporate son throughout the world.

These things have to be the work of the Holy Spirit who is building God's house. *"Except the Lord build the house, they labor in vain who build it"* (Ps. 127:1).

No man knows how to build God's house. Man cannot legislate or institutionalize God's divine order. He can only submit to the sanctifying work of the Holy Spirit who is doing the building and be radically obedient to that particular thing he is shown by the Spirit to do. Any attempt to build, legislate, or institutionalize ahead of the Spirit is carnal, resulting in legalism and death. *"...the letter kills, but the Spirit gives life"* (2 Cor. 3:6).

Rivers of Living Water from Within

These crucified ones are self-starters. The life and power of the Spirit is the driving force within them. They have themselves become that living water welling up from within their innermost being, flowing as rivers of life (John 7:38).

They do not need to be prompted to praise and worship, to pray, to fast, to give, to respond to all that is demanded by the Spirit.

They do not need to run to this seminar on healing or that workshop on deliverance. They will not have to buy all those books and tapes on "how to this" and "how to that."

They will not have to try to grasp the promises of God in their lives through endless incantations of faith con fessions.

The Kingdom of God is within them (Luke 17:21). The Word of God is within them. They are in Him and He is in them. They are one, even as He is one with the Father (John 17:21). The Word of God is the promises of God; therefore, the promises of God are within them and cannot be attained by grasping outwardly for them.

Moreover, they not only have the Kingdom, the Word, the promises, and the Person of the Word within them, they are themselves becoming the manifestation of the word of God in and through their lives. They are *living epistles* (2 Cor. 3:2-3), *oracles* (1 Pet. 4:11). They are the Word made flesh in their own bodies as they are the body of Christ in the world.

Normal Christian Life

This is not to say that these crucified ones are an elite body of people in terms of how the world thinks of elite. On the contrary, they are the subject of much ridicule and disdain in the world.

The crucified life is that to which God has called all of His disciples. It is considered normal Christian living from God's point of view. Any attempt at life in Christ that is less than this is sub-normal, immature discipleship.

Yet, it is not something that one can attain in one's own strength.

Jesus alone is the fulfillment of all the feasts and courts. He is our redeemer and our redemption, our justifier and our justification, our deliverer and our deliverance, our sanctifier and our sanctification, our glorifier and our glorification. If we want any of these things we have to get Him. He is it!

It is not a matter of God being willing to redeem, justify, deliver, sanctify, and glorify. He's already done it. It's a matter of our believing in Him as the finisher of His own work—done on our behalf—and of our being willing for God to work in us all that he has done for us.

Some people are not willing to go on in sanctification and glorification. You cannot have glorification without first going through sanctification. You can not have sanctification without first going through justification. We were justified, we are being sanctified, we will be glorified—together, this is the salvation process. We are becoming who we are in Christ Jesus.

Thus, we not only have all three feasts and courts fulfilled in Jesus, but they are being worked out in our lives as we are willing and yielded. Oswald Chambers, in his devotional book, *My Utmost for His Highest*, wrote, "It is not a question of whether God is willing to sanctify me; is it *my* will? Am I willing to let God do in me all that has been made possible by the Atonement?"

Born out of Fire

These crucified ones are born out of fire. Acts 8:1-4 records an example of this among those first century Christians. Here we read that Saul had consented to Stephen's death; thus great persecution arose against the church in Jerusalem. Because of this persecution, the disciples were scattered abroad throughout the regions of Judea and Samaria, except the apostles. These scattered Christians went forth preaching the word.

Jesus Christ had given those first disciples the commission to *"go...and teach all nations, baptizing them..."* (Matt. 28:19-20), but they were at ease in their Jerusalem cove and were not going out as they had been commissioned. Therefore, it took persecution to scatter them and the word abroad.

I sense that once again, it will take persecution to scatter the saints for the spread of the true gospel.

I say "true" gospel because any gospel that does not preach "Jesus Christ and Him crucified" is not the true but is "another gospel." Social justice, the rebirth experience, holiness, faith, prosperity, church order, and other such teachings may be truths but are not in and of themselves "the" gospel. They may be by-products of the gospel to one extent or the other. But the gospel, according to the apostle Paul, whose writings we hold inspired and sacred, is Christ and Him crucified. 1 Corinthians 2:2: *"For I determined not to know anything among you, save Jesus Christ, and Him crucified."*

Persecution is often God's shaking—His tool for the fulfillment of the great commission.

A Higher Realm in the Spirit

Having gone from Passover through Pentecost, the crucified ones have crossed over into a higher realm in the Spirit, reaching over into Tabernacles even before it's fulfillment. (I will stress again that this higher realm is expected of and available to every true, hungry, seeking disciple.)

We have a type of this in the Old Testament when David and his men ate the consecrated bread (1 Sam. 21:4-

6). In regard to this, Matthew 12:1-8 tells of a time when Jesus and his disciples were walking through a grain field on a Sabbath and ate some of the grain. The Pharisees saw them and questioned Jesus about this unlawful thing they did. Jesus reminded them of how David had entered the house of God and ate the consecrated showbread which he was not permitted by law to do. Yet, he was blameless.

Jesus then declared that something greater than the temple was there. He was referring to Himself—that He was the Lord of the Sabbath. In other words, David, because of his intimate relationship with God, reached beyond the Law and laid hold of the Lord of the Law Himself. He moved in a higher realm in the Spirit.

There is a bread for the children of God of which we have not been privileged to partake until now because we have not yet crossed over into that crucified life for ourselves. We have been operating in the mercy and grace of Him who went in before us once and for all as the Great High Priest: Jesus Christ, Lord.

Once the crucified ones have truly crossed over into the Holy of Holies—the place where Jesus is the only thing there is, where Christ is not only preached as crucified but where the believer himself is a living example of that sacrificial life (Rom. 12:1)—they will have come to a place where they may never be sick, crippled, or diseased again; where demons cannot oppress, torment, or tempt; where material things are irrelevant because these things have nothing to do with a dead man. Moreover, the blessings of God will be in pursuit of them.

Jesus is their pattern. His sacrificial life becomes their lives, and their lives become His. The Holy Spirit gave gifts and ministries as tools to equip the saints for the work of "service" to the end of becoming like Him. We are fast approaching the end and the perfecting of the saints— those who are willing to go through the cross in Christ.

Chapter 3

Consumed

Isn't it interesting that God should appoint feasts (something having to do with eating) as occasions for Israel's worship, as representations of His finished work in Christ, and as representations of the divine relationship we have "in Him."

The Passover Lamb, typifying the death of Jesus Christ who was the Lamb of God without spot or wrinkle, was to be completely eaten by the children of Israel in their dwelling on the night before their departure from Egypt. Any of the flesh (meat) that was not eaten was to be consumed by fire. Either way, the sacrifice had to be completely consumed. (Ex. 12:5,10.)

Later on in ancient Israel, God ordained that the Levitical priests were to eat the offerings of the Lord made by fire and declared that this was their inheritance among their brethren (Josh. 13:14).

God intended from the beginning that the whole nation of Israel was to be a kingdom of priests and a holy nation unto Him (Ex. 19:6). In their failure to obey God, He later appointed the tribe of Levites to minister as priests unto the Lord (Deut. 10:8).

In Christ, all believers have fulfilled God's desire to have for Himself a *"chosen generation, a royal priesthood, a holy nation..."* (1 Peter 2:9). In Christ, God abolished the need for only a few to serve Him as priests and established the priesthood of every believer.

Christ Jesus, the Lamb of God, has become our inheritance as priests. We are to consume Him. In John 6:58, Jesus identified Himself with *"that bread which came down from heaven."* He told His disciples to eat His flesh and drink His blood (John 6:53-56). This was a hard saying, and the scriptures say from that day forward many returned from following after Him (John 6:60-66).

It is one thing to partake of the Lord's supper which commemorates his death, but quite another thing to partake of Him and to participate in His death through our own laid-down life.

As we look at the progression of these feasts as they relate to the three courts of the Tabernacle with particular regard to these crucified ones, we find that four things are to happen to complete the sanctification (separation) process.

Consuming Christ

First, we are to utterly consume Christ. We symbolically represent this in the observance of the Lord's Supper. Matthew 26:26-29 reads, *"And as they were eating, Jesus took bread, and blessed it, and broke it, and gave it to the disciples, and said, 'Take, eat; this is My body.' And he took the cup, and gave thanks, and gave it to them, saying, 'Drink you all of it; for this is My blood of the new testament, which is shed for many for the remission of sins."* (See also Mark 14:22-24; Luke 22:19-20; 1 Cor. 11:24-25.)

The King James Version of the Bible reads, *"Drink ye all of it"* with regard to the cup. The more recent translations read *"Drink of it, all of you."* The Greek syntax leaves this passage somewhat uncertain, "Drink ye of it all." I suggest that the King James Version is in keeping with the Passover when they were instructed to eat all of the lamb, and what was not eaten was to be consumed by fire by the next morning. In both of these ceremonies, the emphasis is upon total consumption. We are to utterly consume Jesus.

To partake of the symbol only is useless ritual unless the participant has first received Jesus, the bread of Life, unto himself. Jesus is received when one is born again (from above) (John 3:3-8).

To eat His flesh and drink His blood is to so consume Christ Jesus as Lord that your very nature is changed. You have become a new creature. *"Therefore if any man is in Christ, he is a new creature: old things are passed away; behold, all things are become new"* (2 Cor. 5:17).

To be baptized in water is a symbol of this baptism into His death, burial, and resurrection. *"Do you not know that as many of us as were baptized into Jesus Christ were baptized into His death? Therefore we are buried with Him by baptism into death: that just as Christ was raised up from the dead by the glory of the Father, even so we also should walk in newness of life"* (Rom. 6:4-5). *"[You are] buried with Him in baptism, wherein also you are risen with Him through the faith of the operation of God, who has raised Him from the dead"* (Col. 2:12). *"For you are dead, and your life is hidden with Christ in God"* (Col. 3:3).

Water baptism covers the ground of our spiritual experience in Christ from death to ascension. *"And [God has] made us sit together in heavenly places in Christ Jesus"* (Eph. 2:6). All of these spiritual experiences precede Pentecost.

Indeed, we are to take <u>all</u> of Him which is the beginning of our heavenly walk with Him.

Consumed by Christ

Secondly, as we utterly consume Him, we find that we are then consumed by Him. It's a mystery to the carnal mind how we can be in Christ and He in us just as He is in the Father. *"At that day"* (after the Comforter, the Holy Spirit, is given on Pentecost) *"you shall know that I am in My Father, and you in Me, and I in you"* (John 14:20).

This unity with the Godhead is still within the realm of Passover where we are redeemed, justified, given eternal life, and ascendancy. To gain Him is to gain eternal life; that is, to be all wrapped up in Him—to be consumed by Him.

To consume Him is to take Him in. To be consumed by Him is to be taken over by Him—to be made one with Him. We take all of Him. He takes all of us.

Consumed with Christ

But there's more that needs to happen. We consume Him in order to be consumed by Him that we might be consumed with Him. This is where Pentecost comes down upon us.

John told those coming out to be baptized in water that one was coming *"whose shoes I am not worthy to bear: He shall baptize you in the Holy Ghost and fire"* (Matt. 3:11).

Pentecost was the fulfillment of this promise. *"And, being assembled together with them, [Jesus] commanded them that they should not depart from Jerusalem, but wait for the promise of the Father, which, He said, you have heard of Me. For John truly baptized with water; but you shall be baptized with the Holy Ghost not many days hence"* (Acts 1:4-5).

On the day of Pentecost, Peter explained that this was that which Joel had prophesied would come to pass in the last days. *"I will pour out My Spirit upon all flesh..."* (Acts 2:17).

In Passover we get Jesus. Jesus means Savior. In Pentecost we get Christ. Christ means "the anointed one." Christ is the Greek translation for the Hebrew word, Messiah.

The Holy Spirit is the anointing power of Christ's ministry in and through His disciples. <u>We are given the Holy Spirit mainly to give us the power of His lordship. Without the Holy Spirit we are unable to do the work of God.</u>

To be baptized in the Holy Spirit is to be utterly consumed with God in Christ—to be soaked, saturated, infiltrated, immersed with the great and glorious Holy Spirit of God Almighty. Those who are so baptized have Him as the abundance of their hearts. They hunger and thirst for more and more of Him. He is their preoccupation. They eat, drink, sleep, think Jesus. Consumed with Him!

Further, they are given over to that fire of the Holy Spirit which is separating them from sin, the world, the flesh, and all the domain of Satan. They are submitted to His refiner's fire in order to gain that *"holiness [sanctification] without which no man shall see the Lord"* (Heb. 12:14).

The Holy Spirit is given that we might be led of Him, be taught of Him, minister to Him in the high praises of God for which He is worthy—that we might worship Him in Spirit and truth, that we might have the power of His Lordship, that we might bear the fruit of the Spirit, that we might be witnesses unto Him in the uttermost parts of the earth, that we might be to the praise of His glory, and, ultimately, that we might be conformed into the image of His Son, Jesus Christ, our Lord.

In Pentecost, then, we are sanctified but not yet satisfied. For the goal of Passover and Pentecost is the fulfillment of Tabernacles. The whole creation is still groaning for the revealing of the sons of God. *"For the earnest expectation of the creation waits for the manifestation [revealing] of the sons of God"* (Rom. 8:19-23).

A Consuming Fire for Christ

We are to consume Him and be consumed by Him that we might be consumed with Him <u>that, finally, we might be a consuming fire for Him.</u>

"Our God is a consuming fire" (Heb. 12:29), and that is what all true believers have been called to be as well: a consuming fire. Whoever becomes a consuming fire, by the very nature of their laid-down lives, will become an offense to the world, the flesh, and Satan.

They will become the target of persecution. Did Jesus not Himself warn, *"If the world hates you, you know that it hated Me before it hated you. If you were of the world, the world would love its own: but because you are not of the world, but I have chosen you out of the world, therefore the world hates you. The servant is not greater than his lord. If they have persecuted Me, they will also persecute you..."* (John 15:18-20).

We read in the Bible that the glory of the Lord filled the house of the Lord only three times: The Tabernacle of Moses (Ex. 40:34), Solomon's temple (1 Kings 8:11), and Ezekiel's temple (Ezek. 10:4; 43:4-5; 44:4).

I believe Ezekiel's temple represents this end-time army of believers coming forth in this latter day. We are the temple of the Holy Spirit (1 Cor. 6:19). It will be this house of many sons that the glory of the Lord will once again fill.

The glory never returned to Zerubbabel's or Herod's temple. It has been reserved for this final period before the coming of the Lord when many sons will be brought to glory. *"For it became Him, for whom are all things, and by whom are all things, in bringing many sons to glory, to make the captain of their salvation perfect through sufferings"* (Heb. 2:10).

In Passover we are redeemed and justified; in Pentecost we are being sanctified; in Tabernacles we will be glorified. That will be completed when Jesus comes. But as I say, there is a foretaste of that coming now, and forerunners are coming forth in the spirit of Elijah, preparing the way of the Lord's second coming (Mal. 4:5).

It is said of dieting that you are what you eat. So it is with spiritual things.

To eat His flesh and drink His blood is to partake of His righteousness and thereby become the righteousness of God.

To eat His flesh and drink His blood is to partake of His holiness and thereby become the holiness of God.

To eat His flesh and drink His blood is to partake of His glory and thereby become the glory of God.

To eat His flesh and drink His blood is to partake of His divine nature and thereby become the nature of the divine.

To eat His flesh and drink His blood is to become "broken bread and poured out wine" (to borrow from Oswald Chambers).

Chapter 4

Redemption/Justification

Because of the blood atonement of Jesus we <u>are</u> justified and redeemed, we <u>are being</u> sanctified (separated unto God from sin, Satan, flesh, and the world), and we <u>will be</u> glorified. To better understand this process of salvation, let's turn now to a brief look at our redemption and justification.

Christ Is Our Redeemer/Justifier

God will never pet our flesh; He puts it to death. He will never nurse <u>our</u> causes—He is interested only in His cause.

His cause is the redemption of mankind. You can't receive this redemption through any other way or door but through the blood atonement of Jesus Christ.

You cannot be redeemed and justified by the works of the Law. The Law was not given to redeem men from sin but to convict them of it. Conviction alone cannot save. We must add repentance to conviction. Repentance means to turn away, turn around, do an about-face, change our thinking. But we can't just turn away from wrong. We must turn toward the Redeemer.

The Law tells us what is right. The Law is the basis for all righteous judgment. The Law has to be satisfied with righteousness; that is, the Law has to be obeyed perfectly. It is impossible to accomplish this in the fallen, cursed nature of human flesh. Jesus, on the other hand, being the perfect Son of God, accomplished the righteous requirement of the Law.

"For He has made Him to be sin for us, who knew no sin; that we might be made the righteousness of God in

25

Him" (2 Cor. 5:21).

"Christ has redeemed us from the curse of the Law, being made a curse for us: for it is written, 'Cursed is every one who hangs on a tree'" (Gal. 3:13).

God may give you a work to do. But your works will never redeem you. Your redemption is past tense: accomplished in Christ Jesus. The Law has been satisfied by the blood of the Lamb.

The only way to get in on this satisfaction is through faith in the Redeemer—faith that He has saved, redeemed, justified, healed, delivered; that He is sanctifying; that He will glorify. It is faith in His finished work. He is the Savior, the Redeemer, the Justifier.

We are justified by faith.

Humility

This is a humbling relationship we have with our Redeemer—for we cannot save ourselves or in any sense improve upon ourselves so as to make ourselves more acceptable. The more acceptable we try to make ourselves, the less acceptable we become. The more unacceptable we realize we are, the better positioned we are to be forgiven and to put our trust in Him who has redeemed us. We are neither able to save ourselves or others.

It is through humility and brokenness that we enter into the Kingdom of God. Jesus humbled Himself to the point that He, *"being in the form of God, thought it not robbery to be equal with God: But made Himself of no reputation, and took upon Him the form of a servant..."* (Phil. 2:6-7).

His humility did not negate His Godship. Rather, through it, He shows us the way to Him. He is the example. His whole humanity was given that we might see God, know God, and come unto God.

Because of Jesus who met us on our level, we are able now to approach God. That is why Hebrews 12:18-24 says we have *"not come to the mount that might be touched..."* but *"unto Mount Zion..."* That is to say, we have not come to the Law, but to grace. We have not come to wrath, but to mercy.

Therefore, let us not continue to frustrate the grace of God by sinning when we, through the blood of Jesus, have been set free from the bondage to sin.

Jesus is the door of the sheep. Any man who tries to enter in by any other door is a thief and a robber (John 10:1,9).

Altar of Burnt Sacrifice

The outer court with the altar of burnt sacrifice upon which the animals were slain foreshadowed this Redeemer God who came in the likeness of man to shed His precious blood as an atonement for the sins of the world— the Lamb of God without spot or blemish.

Of this Lamb, John wrote in Revelation 5:9, *"And they sang a new song, saying, 'You are worthy to take the book, and to open the seals thereof: for you were slain, and have redeemed us to God by your blood out of every kindred, and tongue, and people, and nation.'"*

Jesus, the Lamb of God, was the Word made flesh (John 1:1,14). The word of God is the Law of God. Through His birth, His sanctified life, His death, burial, and resurrection, He, being the Law, fulfilled or satisfied the righteous requirement of the Law.

"For by grace are you saved through faith; and that not of yourselves: it is the gift of God" (Eph. 2:8-10).

Laver of Brass

Between the tabernacle and the altar of burnt offerings was placed a laver of brass. Water was put into it, and the priests were to wash their hands and their feet from it before entering the tabernacle of the congregation or before they came near the altar to minister the burnt offerings unto the Lord (Ex. 30:17-21).

I believe this washing was foreshadowing water baptism under the new covenant. *"Be baptized every one of you in the name of Jesus Christ for the remission [forgiveness] of sins..."* (Acts 2:38). The apostle Paul was recounting his conversion experience during his defense in Jerusalem when he quoted Ananias as having said, *"...Arise, and be baptized, and wash away your sins, calling on the name of the Lord"* (Acts 22:16).

Having been saved, redeemed, justified, and <u>cleansed</u> by the sacrificed life of Jesus and the shedding of His blood, we have been born again (John 3:3,7), have been made new creatures in Christ Jesus (2 Cor. 5:17), and have that divine deposit of eternal life within us (John 6:47).

We have been birthed into the kingdom of God, we are babes in Christ, children of God, heirs and joint heirs with Christ, living in Father God's house—sons of God, brothers and sisters in the Lord. Water baptism is essentially associated with this outer court ministry. There is more on baptism in chapter five.

Redemption: the Beginning of Salvation

That we are redeemed by the blood of the Lamb is the evangelical message of the church to the world. Redemption is the beginning of salvation to which we have all been called.

Jesus Christ is our redeemer, our justifier, and our savior who became the propitiation (appeasement, conciliation) for our sins—our substitute on the cross.

We believe in Him. We put our trust in Him. We abide in Him as He abides in us, and through Him we have eternal life with the Father. Nothing can be taken from this reality. This is the beginning of our salvation.

But there is a perfecting of the saints that God wants to bring about in His people; a going on from faith to faith, glory to glory; a growing up into Him. The Bible views us who believe as God's building. This analogy helps us understand just how redemption is the beginning of His salvation process.

But God has a plan for building His house. God the Father is the Great Architect of His building. He alone holds the blueprint. *"Except the Lord build the house, they labor in vain who build it..."* (Ps. 127:1).

We are God's house, His building (1 Cor. 3:9), lively stones (1 Pet. 2:5), building itself up in love (Eph. 4:16).

We are also co-builders with the Holy Spirit of God who is the contractor and administrator of God's building project.

Jesus is the pattern so that when the house is finished we will all look like Him (Eph. 4:13).

The ultimate goal of redemption is for Christ to be formed in us (Gal. 4:19).

The equipping gift ministries of apostles, prophets, evangelists, pastors and teachers are given to perfect the saints for the work of ministry, for the building up of the body of Christ (Eph. 4:11-12). The gifts of the Spirit (1 Cor. 12) are given as tools for service in this perfecting, building-up process.

These tools will pass away. They are not ends in themselves but are instruments in God's hand to complete His divine purposes with all mankind. Once His house is built, the tools will pass away. The perfect will have come (1 Cor. 13:10). The perfect is that *"perfect [many-membered] man, unto [patterned after] the measure of the stature of the fullness of Christ"* (Eph. 4:13).

"For we are [God's] workmanship, created in Christ Jesus unto good works, which God has before ordained that we should walk in them" (Eph. 2:10).

Just as Jesus was the pattern for us, once we take in His divine nature, we are to take on His divine nature that we might be living epistles: *"You are our epistle written in our hearts, known and read of men: forasmuch as you are manifestly declared to be the epistle of Christ ministered by us, written not with ink, but with the Spirit of the living God; not in tables of stone, but in fleshly tables of the heart"* (2 Cor. 3:2-3).

The Greater Works of God

We are His body—His feet, His hands, His mouth, His heart, His mind—in the world today. We are to carry on as He did on the earth, the exception being that we not only have the calling of His earthly ministry but the power of His ascendancy as well—that is, the gift of the Spirit. As He said, *"...It is expedient for you that I go away: for if I go not away, the Comforter will not come unto you; but if I depart, I will send Him unto you"* (John 16:7).

Knowing this beforehand, He declared, *"...He that believes on Me, the works that I do shall he do also; and greater works than these shall he do; because I go unto My Father"* (John 14:12).

We are the greater works of God—not just in what we do—for it seems unlikely that we can do greater than He. But the greater works we do is certainly the greater works He's done, is doing, and shall accomplish in us in His work of redemption, sanctification, and glorification.

We <u>are</u> *"to the praise of His glory"* (Eph. 1:6,12,14), not by our works, but by His works within us.

Therefore, the lives that we live as crucified ones, we *"live by the faith of the Son of God who loved [us] and gave Himself for [us]"* (Gal. 2:20).

Therefore, if we expect to be in this company of crucified ones, He beseeches us by His mercies to present our bodies as living sacrifices, holy and acceptable unto Him, which is our reasonable service (Rom. 12:1).

We are Him in the world—ambassadors (2 Cor. 5:20). Our very lives are to reflect the power of His Lordship to convict others of sin and call them to repentance, that they too might enter into the way, the truth, and the life (John 14:6)—Jesus Christ as Lord.

Chapter 5

Sanctification

There is more to God's call in our lives than to merely receive His redemption so we can go to heaven when we die. Consider this:

The true church is an obedient people.

This is a hard but true saying. To eat His flesh and drink His blood (John 6:53-56) is to utterly lay down our lives for Him to accomplish His absolute and perfect will in our lives. Nothing else matters.

The true servant is Jesus. Jesus was absolutely devoted to accomplishing His Father's will. It was Father's will that led Jesus into Gethsemane. It was Father's will that led Him before Caiaphas and Pilate. It was Father's will that nailed Him to a cruel Roman cross. It was Father's will that He die upon the cross and shed His undefiled blood for the sins of a defiled world.

The true church—those who are true disciples—are those who bear the brand-marks of His servanthood (Gal. 6:17), who so render their own vessels dead to sin that He can reign and rule as sovereign Lord in their lives.

The true church is an obedient people.

Three Dimensions of Man

There are three dimensions to man. He is a living soul with a spirit and dwells in a fleshly body. He has been redeemed in his spirit. He is being renewed in his soul which consists of his mind, will, and emotions. But his fleshly body is corrupt and fallen and is subject only to the grave and decay. Only in that great resurrection of the dead will the holy ones of God be redeemed in their bodies. At that

31

time, they shall receive for themselves their glorified bodies (1 Cor. 15:35-50).

These three dimensions are all touched by the three feasts of Israel and the three courts of the Tabernacle. Working from the inside out, the spirit of man is redeemed and justified in the fulfillment of Passover. The soul (personality) of man is being renewed day by day, sanctified, in the fulfillment of Pentecost. Then, in the fulfillment of Tabernacles, when His holy ones are caught up in the air and gathered into Him, they will receive their glorified bodies (1 Cor. 15:49,52).

The only healings of our present human bodies are temporary: *"Though our outward man perish, yet the inward man is renewed day by day"* (2 Cor. 4:16).

Growing Up

It is this inner man of the soul (personality) of which I now speak, whose human spirit has been redeemed.

Having been redeemed, he has become a new creature in Christ Jesus (2 Cor. 5:17). He is a babe in Christ. He is to *"grow up into Him in all things, who is the head, even Christ"* (Eph. 4:15). A maturation is expected.

He is to grow up into Him; that is, into Christ Jesus. He is to take on the nature of His Father. He is to be conformed into the image of the Son (Rom. 8:29). He is being transformed by the renewing of his mind that He may prove what is the acceptable and perfect will of the Father (Rom. 12:2).

A process has begun in him that is intended to bring him onward and upward into the high calling of God in Christ (Phil. 3:14).

There is only one way he can come into this upward calling and that is through the baptism in the Holy Spirit and fire. Thus, we leave the outer court of Passover and go into the Holy Place of Pentecost, carrying with us the sacrificial blood of the Lamb. For we now need the power of His Lordship working in us.

Three Baptisms

In a sense we have three baptisms. Hebrews 6:1-2 reads, *"Therefore leaving the principles of the doctrine of*

Christ, *let us go on unto perfection;* not laying again the foundation of repentance from dead works, and of faith toward God, of the doctrine of *baptisms*..." Notice the plural on baptisms.

1. Baptism in water

We are baptized in water which is our first act of obedience having come to Christ in faith. The children of Israel symbolized this when they crossed over the Red Sea from Egypt (the world) into the wilderness (a time of testing and preparation). The scriptures explain, they *"were all baptized into Moses"* (1 Cor. 10:2). The laver for cleansing in the outer court represents this baptism (washing) upon redemption.

Those witnessing Pentecost asked what must they do. Peter answered plainly, *"Repent, and be baptized everyone of you in the name of Jesus Christ for the remission of sins..."* (Acts 2:38). This is the first thing every new believer must do.

Water baptism is associated with the washing away of sins. In Acts 22:16, the apostle Paul is testifying to his conversion and how that Ananias charged him, *"Arise, and be baptized, and wash away your sins, calling on the name of the Lord."*

Any believer can baptize another believer in water. Water baptism represents our baptism into Jesus—into His death, burial, and resurrection (Rom. 6:4).

2. Baptism in the Holy Spirit

This second baptism, the baptism in the Holy Spirit, can only be done by Jesus Himself. John the Baptist proclaimed that, *"I indeed baptize you in water unto repentance: but He that comes after me...He shall baptize you in the Holy Ghost and fire"* (Matt. 3:11).

This first occurred on the day of Pentecost as described in Acts 2. Jesus Himself told them to wait in Jerusalem until they received the promise of the Father at which time they would be baptized (immersed) in the Holy Ghost (Acts 1:4-5). *"But you shall receive power, after that the Holy Ghost has come upon you..."* (Acts 1:8).

The Holy Spirit is given for the explicit purpose of giving us the power of His Lordship. If Jesus Christ is to be Lord in deed and not in word only, one must be empowered with the Holy Ghost; one must of necessity be immersed in the Holy Spirit of God. That's where the power is. One must of necessity go on from the outer court of Passover to the Holy Place of Pentecost.

If one expects this renewal process, this growing up into Him to take place, he must humble himself and receive this immersion in His Spirit.

It is not enough to learn more and more Bible. It's not enough to have well-defined doctrines. It's not enough to be religious even in your daily life. It's not enough to hear eloquent sermons on Sunday, sing in the choir, teach Sunday School, visit the sick, and so on and on.

Unless a change is transpiring within the soul of man, unless he is being brought to perfection, to holiness from within, he will not see the Lord.

Those who refuse this baptism will have to be content to be numbered among those of whom the scriptures speak, *"Having a form of godliness, but denying the power thereof..."* (2 Tim. 3:5).

3. Baptism of His sufferings

We are first baptized into Jesus as expressed through the outward act of water baptism. Secondly, we are baptized in the Holy Spirit and fire that we might have His power to go on into His Lordship. Then, thirdly, through this baptism in the Holy Spirit and fire, the way is made for us to be baptized into His sufferings. It is a sharing in His sufferings. The Holy Spirit performs the baptism of suffering in our lives.

Matthew 20:20-23 tells about the time when the mother of James and John asked Jesus if He would grant that her sons would sit one on His right hand and one on His left hand in His Kingdom. Jesus answered, *"'You don't know what you ask. Are you able to drink of the cup that I shall drink of, and to be baptized with the baptism that I am baptized with?' They said to him, 'We are able.' And He said to them, 'You shall drink indeed of My cup, and be baptized with the baptism that I am baptized with...'"*

Jesus was not mincing words here. They very well understood that this baptism had to do with a suffering unto death, a participation with Him in His death (Matt. 20:18).

Such is the consecration of overcomers. *"And they overcame him [Satan] by the blood of the Lamb, and by the word of their testimony; and they loved not their lives unto the death"* (Rev. 12:11).

According to Luke 22:31-34, Jesus warned Peter that Satan had asked for him that he might sift him as wheat. He then comforted Peter by telling him that he had prayed for him that his faith should not fail.

Peter boasted, *"Lord, I am ready to go with you, both to prison and to death."* Peter really believed that he was ready.

Then Jesus told Peter that before the cock crowed three times that day he would deny Him. And three times Peter did deny Him.

In John 21:15-19, we see that Jesus restored Peter. The original Greek wording of this event reveals something very interesting between the two of them.

First, Jesus asked Peter if he loved him. The Greek word *agapeo* is used for this love which carries with it the idea of self-denial.

The Greek word that is used to convey Peter's answer was *phileo* which has a more brotherly, affectionate, soulish, self-interest meaning to it. He did not answer with the self-denial kind of love.

A second time Jesus asked, *"Simon, son of Jonah, do you love [agapeo] me?"*

The second time Peter answered with *phileo* as if to say, "You know I love you affectionately."

Then the third time Jesus asked, *"Do you love [phileo] me?"* As if to ask, is that all?

Having already failed once, Simon could no longer make such a boast as is involved in *agapeo*. He could only answer with affectionate love.

Simon wanted so much to be able to say, "Yea, Lord," but he knew there was nothing within his own strength to make such a vow.

Then, precious Jesus said to Peter (vv. 18-19), *"'Truly, truly, I say to you, when you were young, you girded yourself and walked where you wished; but when you are old, you shall stretch forth your hands, and another shall gird you and carry you where you do not wish.' This He spoke signifying by what death he would glorify God. And when He had spoken this, He said to him, 'Follow Me.'"*

Jesus was not simply asking Peter to follow Him out of the room. He was calling him to follow Him unto death.

Peter's previous boasting later became God's promise. And after all was said and done in Peter's life and ministry, he not only went to prison but to death, following his Lord in this baptism of suffering. However, he did not go through this baptism in his own time or strength—only in God's!

Jesus learned obedience by the things which He suffered (Heb. 5:8). *"And being found in fashion as a man, He humbled Himself, and became obedient unto death, even the death of the cross"* (Phil. 2:8).

We are being brought to obedience, to servanthood, to sonship through the things we suffer, through our participation in His sufferings.

Children, Sons, and Fathers

With regard to our being brought into sonship, we once again see things unfolding in threes. Three in the Bible generally is the number that speaks of the fullness of testimony.

1 John 2:12-14 speaks of children, sons, and fathers. Fathers are children-centered. They care for the children. Sons are father-centered. They care for the things of father. They want to fulfill his will. But children are typically self-centered. And so it is in the Kingdom of God.

Those who remain in the outer court are children. Those who go on to the Holy Place are sons. And those who reach the realm of maturity in the Holy of Holies take on the nature of Father. They are Abrahams.

Having been a child, we never lose that childlike nature. It is the only way we can come into the Kingdom. We are born into it as babes. Having been a son, we never lose that. Even as fathers we remain privileged as children in Father-God's house, and we remain servants as sons in Father-God's house. All three natures remain. But we are to grow up into Him.

"When I was a child, I spoke as a child, I understood as a child, I thought as a child: but when I became a man, I put away childish things" (1 Cor. 13:11).

Baptism in the Holy Spirit

As children, we are self-centered. We are subject to the discipline of the Lord to bring us to maturity (Heb. 12:5-11).

If we willfully despise this discipline and thereby reject God's process to grow us up into Him, we shall remain self-centered and self-seeking and thereby miss the whole idea of discipleship.

If we are self-seeking, we are carnal, fleshly.

If we are fleshly, then we are idolaters. We worship ourselves and are given to our own wills instead of God's.

If we are idolaters, then we are harlots. All idolatry in the Bible is viewed as spiritual harlotry—going after other gods. Spiritual harlotry is anything for self.

Consider who Christ is coming for when He returns. He is coming for "a glorious church, not having spot, or wrinkle, or any such thing; but that it should be holy and without blemish" (Eph. 5:27). He is coming for a people who have been separated from sin, self, the world, and the domain of Satan. The bride is the one of whom Revelation 19:7 speaks, "...His wife has made herself ready."

Christ is not coming for the harlot nor for a people with harlot hearts. He is not coming for a rebellious bride. He is coming for and will gather up unto Himself those who have eyes only for Him, who are radically intent upon following Him wherever He goes (Rev. 14:4).

The true church is an obedient people.

The only way one can come to this place of obedience is through the baptism in the Holy Spirit and fire. It is the baptism "in" the Holy Spirit. We are immersed, filled, soaked, saturated, consumed in the Holy Spirit of God.

Who wouldn't want that/Him! And He's all for the asking if the intent of our hearts is right.

It is not a doctrine to be debated or an experience to be sought after or rejected. The baptism is a relationship with God in the power of His Holy, divine Spirit.

He, the Spirit of truth, is the force that projects us onward into the high calling of God in Christ. You cannot get to the Holy of Holies of Tabernacles without first doing service in the Holy Place of Pentecost.

Baptism in water takes place in the outer court of Passover. The baptism in the Holy Spirit and fire takes place in the Holy Place of Pentecost. Both baptisms have as their ultimate spiritual goal to bring us to the only baptism that really counts—the baptism into Jesus where we are wholly, totally crucified with Him and raised up in Him—where we have become, as it were, Him.

"I am crucified with Christ: nevertheless I live; yet not I, but Christ lives in me: and the life which I now live in the flesh I live by the faith of the Son of God, who loved me, and gave Himself for me" (Gal. 2:20).

To be baptized in the Holy Spirit of God is to be filled with His praise, His power, His purposes, His plans, His program, His perfecting processes, His purging, His purifying...His everything.

This is the sanctification process without which we shall not see the Lord (Heb. 12:14).

Passover, Pentecost, and Tabernacles Compared

Before leaving this chapter, let us see how this sanctification process fits into the three feast days.

Healing and deliverance are given in Passover (not in Pentecost as many Pentecostals assume). Passover is the cross. The cross is the laid-down life. Many are preaching a salvation without the cross. Yet, there is no salvation apart from the cross; that is, the laid-down life. To preach a salvation without the cross is not the true gospel.

Pentecost is the power of Passover. We must be baptized (immersed) in the Holy Spirit and fire for us to live the crucified life. The indwelling Holy Spirit is our ability to walk in the Lordship of Jesus Christ.

Passover without Pentecost is law. Jesus is the law written in our hearts. He is also the ability in us to live according to that perfect law of liberty. Thus He gave us His Holy Spirit that we might be clothed with power from on high. To accept the Jesus of Passover and reject the Holy Spirit of Pentecost is to know what is right and not have the power to do what is right. Therefore, we are left under the law. It remains for us to do what is right in our own strength.

Pentecost, however, without Passover is deception. When we do not understand that Pentecost is the power of Passover, we tend to go for the "blessing." We seek the gifts for the sake of having the gifts. These become ends in themselves. But the gift of the Holy Spirit is given that we might know Him (Jesus) and the power of His resurrection.

Pentecost will always point onward to Tabernacles, which is the fullness of Passover; that is, the cross and the laid-down life.

Healing and deliverance without the cross is superficial. We are not healed and delivered because we are baptized (immersed) in the Holy Spirit and fire, but because we have died and our lives are hidden with Christ in God (Col. 3:3).

Tabernacles is being gathered into Jesus. We are seeing the first fruits of that historical event now. We have had the fulfillment of Passover and Pentecost, but have as yet to witness the fulfillment of Tabernacles.

Tabernacles is the goal or completion of Passover made possible by Pentecost. Salvation comes at the end. It is consummated in Tabernacles.

Chapter 6

Agape: The Crucified Life

God's Love to Man

The Christian believer is one who is in divine relationship with God.

This relationship is birthed in the Spirit of God and has its basis in the love of God.

God's love was sacrificial. Christ Jesus Himself gave ultimate meaning to the Greek word for love, *agape.* It is a love that gives until it has no need to give more. It is a love that goes beyond one's own self-centered interest.

"For God so loved the world that He gave His only begotten Son, that whosoever believes in Him should not perish, but have everlasting life" (John 3:16).

God so loved that He gave the ultimate—He gave Himself.

God's ultimate will is to impart His divine life and nature into His created ones so that they might be as He is: holy and righteous.

Lest man should be lifted up in his own personal estimation as being worth anything, God based His salvation of man on His own love, mercy, and grace. When we are totally dependent upon God that way, we can never conclude within ourselves that we are in any wise gods.

God chose to save us from ourselves—we who are bent on self-destruction—by so loving us, by so completely giving of Himself, and that while we were completely undeserving (Rom. 5:8).

This, then, is the basis for *agape:* that one should give in grace and mercy of his life to another who is undeserving.

41

Man's Love to God

Having been made worthy by the blood of the Lamb, having been filled with the life and power of God through the divine impartation of His Holy Spirit, we are given a deeper dimension to the meaning of *agape.*

Having now the example of perfect God giving Himself in mercy and grace to imperfect man, imperfect man is now called upon, even commanded, to give in return of himself to perfect God. Man was undeserving of God's *agape.* But God, to the contrary, is most worthy of our *agape.*

"I beseech you therefore, brethren, by the mercies of God, that you present your bodies a living sacrifice, holy, acceptable unto God, which is your reasonable service" (Rom. 12:1).

God presented Himself upon the cross as a sacrifice unto death—giving until He had no need to give more. We are to present ourselves to Him as a sacrifice unto life—giving of our all until we can give no more.

We are to give up our self-life by our participation into His death and burial (Rom. 6:4) in order for His life to be lived in and through us (Gal. 2:20).

So the only valid, life-producing relationship we can have with God that is acceptable to God is that which is based upon *agape.* He showed us the way. *"Greater love has no man than this, that a man lay down his life for his friends"* (John 15:13). Even then, the love we give to God can only be that love He first imparted to us. It's His love working through us.

Man's Love to Man

Now this *agape* becomes the basis for our relationship with all others in the family of God and beyond. We are to follow His example of the laid-down life. We are to so love one another in mercy and grace so as to impart His very life in one another. His love in us and through us is life-producing. No other form of life can produce eternal life. All other life is material, physical, corruptible.

This is the difference between flesh and spirit: God is spirit. He speaks spirit. He reproduces spirit and does this by His Spirit. Flesh is corruptible, earthly, temporal. Spirit is incorruptible, heavenly, and eternal. Flesh leads to death. Spirit leads to life. Flesh is bondage. Spirit is liberty. Flesh is selfish. Spirit is selfless.

Let us regard one another, especially those of us in the household of God, with this *agape* whereby we so love one another that we give until there's no need to give more. For such giving, such loving is the greatest witness needed by a sinner-world. *"By this shall all men know that you are My disciples, if you have love one to another"* (John 13:35).

We are drawn to that Christ nature of *agape* within each other.

The Obedience of Agape

Now when we so love God and so love our fellow man, we will be operating in the realm of the Spirit. For the only way to truly love with the love of God is to be in the Spirit of God in order to find out how this love is worked out in life.

God alone knows the heart of man. God alone knows what is best to do in each given situation in life. God alone is the solution to every need.

So the faithful are those who deny themselves of their own opinions to find out God's opinion, who deny themselves of their own desires to find out God's desire, who deny themselves of their own wills to find out God's will. The faithful are those who take up their cross, deny themselves (that is, die to self-will) daily, and follow after what God is doing.

They are those who say what God is saying, do what God is doing, and are what God has made them to be. They are true prophets of God; that is, true spokesmen for God by the very life they live. They are living epistles, oracles of God.

Once a believer has become so related to God in *agape,* he has stepped over the line. He has moved from the realm of the flesh over into the realm of the Spirit—not just in talk, but in his walk.

His relationship with God is no more based on self— what he can get from God, but is now founded on God—

what he can give to God.

But what can he give to God in the face of so great a salvation so rich and free? The answer: himself—"a living sacrifice, holy and acceptable unto God..." (Rom. 12:1).

There is nothing we can ever do for God that will ever bear fruit for God except what God, by His Spirit, commands. God has a plan. He has a plan for every man. That plan cannot be carried out in the flesh. It can only be achieved in, with, and by the Holy Spirit of God.

The only true New Testament order for the church is Jesus. He is not a form of government, although He has government. He is not a set of creeds, confessionals, and belief systems; although He sets forth sound doctrines, precepts, and principles to be adhered to. The true church is an obedient people in right relationship with their God.

Jesus never did anything except what He saw or heard the Father do or say (John 5:19-20,30; 12:49). He, in turn, gave us the Holy Spirit and said of Him, "...He shall not speak of Himself; but whatsoever He shall hear, that shall He speak: and He will show you things to come" (John 16:13).

To build what God is building requires that the builder get in touch with God through His Holy Spirit. "As many as are led by the Spirit of God, they are the sons of God" (Rom. 8:14).

The faithful are those who want only to build what God is building. They love Him that much. "If a man love Me, he will keep My words..." (John 14:23).

The faithful are those who want the best of God for their brothers and sisters in the family of God. The only way to know what is best is to find out from Father.

The Fellowship of Agape

Such faithfulness, such agape, such obedience, such relatedness to God can only come through extended times of prayer and fellowship with God. The only way to build any kind of a relationship with anyone is to spend time together. The more time together, the broader the basis becomes for that relationship.

I have children who live away in another town. When I

spend time with them, I find I have more things to talk to them about because we learn more about what's going on in each other's lives. But the less time we spend together, the less we seem to have to say to each other. You think it would work the other way around, but it doesn't.

The more time we spend with God in prayer and in His word—talking and listening—the more we learn of Him, His ways, His desires/will, His purposes in our lives, His blessings upon us—it's endless because He's endless. The more we visit, the more we have to talk about.

The Deeper Walk of Agape

So this is a look into Tabernacles. *"When He shall appear, we shall be like Him; for we shall see Him as He is"* (1 John 3:2). This is that upward call of God (Phil. 3:14), that higher realm in the Spirit, that deeper walk with God, that coming up to Mount Zion: to be like Him.

"Come and let us go up to the mountain of the Lord, to the house of our God. And He will teach us His ways, and we will walk in His paths, for out of Zion shall go forth the law and the word of the Lord from Jerusalem" (Is. 2:3, Micah 4:2).

Zion speaks of a place in God by the Spirit where Jesus is the only thing there is. He is all in all.

Jerusalem speaks of the church, the assembly of called-out ones who are gathered into Jesus.

Once we go to Zion, we become the Zion of God. Once we are given the word, we become the word from Zion: that is, from us shall go forth the law and the word

As long as Jesus fed and healed their flesh, the multitudes followed Him. But those who followed Him to the mountaintops for that deeper instruction in discipleship were few.

We find that the ministries with a reputation for moving in the gifts can pack the house. But few are interested in hearing the word that calls for that sacrificial life of *agape.*

I once had a Christian brother tell me, "You can't build anything upon the cross." He's absolutely right. Nothing of the flesh can be built upon the preaching of the cross.

You have to preach another gospel to get that kind of building done.

But the preaching of the cross is the only preaching that builds the house of God, that accomplishes the great commission of the gospel of the Kingdom.

Some years before this writing, I had the Spirit of the Lord indicate to me that "this gospel of the Kingdom" was not yet being preached throughout the world as Jesus said it would be in Matthew 24:14.

I thought, "But God, with all the TV ministries and missionaries going out...?"

And it came to me again, "I said, 'This gospel of the Kingdom...'"

I knew it was true. There was a form of the gospel, a semblance, or something we thought to be the gospel that was being preached. I could even see that God was working to save souls anyway. But I knew something was missing. This gospel that Jesus talked about was not yet being preached.

I wasn't sure at that time what "this gospel" was. I'm seeing it more clearly today as I see these "crucified ones" coming forth. They not only preach the crucified lifestyle but live it.

Some are living it and don't even know how to talk about it yet. Some are seeing it and trying to describe it but are not necessarily walking it. Ultimately, though, no one can talk of this realm until they are walking in it.

You who read this word and hunger for that deeper walk can have it, whether you see it now or not, by simply asking God to take control and bring you into that Holy of Holies, into the throne room with Him, into that life of holiness before Him, into *agape* —the crucified life.

Chapter 7

Glorification: From Glory to Glory

We are not redeemed, sanctified, and glorified for ourselves, but for God. It is His redemption, not ours; His sanctification, not ours; His glorification, not ours. Though we accrue the benefits of fulfilling His purposes in all history, we must come to the stark realization that He purchased us, we did not purchase Him. We are not our own (1 Cor. 6:19-20). We are His possession, vessels in His hand to do with as He pleases.

When we come to this reality, we will have come to understand what it means to be crucified with Him. Just as Jesus had to come to the end of Himself, emptying Himself (Phil. 2:7 NAS) in order for God to be glorified through Him, so are we to follow Him in His baptism; that is, allow the Holy Spirit to bring us to the end of ourselves that God might be glorified through us.

To the Praise of His Glory

It always happens, though, that when we bring glory to God, God bestows His glory upon us. We are to the praise of His glory (Eph. 1:6,12).

The only way we can be to the praise of His glory is to bring glory to Him. The only way we can bring glory to Him is through our laid-down life. *"Humble yourselves in the sight of the Lord, and He shall lift you up"* (James 4:10).

Everything we do, we do for Him that He may be satisfied, that He may be glorified. This is not to say that we do anything to satisfy God for our salvation. Only Jesus satisfied God for that. Having received redemption, however, we are so given to Him that He lives His life through us.

47

The more He lives His life through us, the more He is glorified and the more we become like Him. Thus, the more we become like Him, the more we share in His glory.

So, it continues to hold that whoever loses His life for Christ's sake shall find it. If you lose your life in Him, you will be found in Him. Since He is the resurrection and the life, that is the only place to be found—in Him.

Being Properly Related

This brings us back to the need to be in proper relationship with God. We need to cultivate this relationship with God. The more we are rightly related to Him, the more we will walk in fellowship and harmony with Him.

He is our peacemaker. He is our righteousness, our justification, our redemption, our sanctification, our provision, our healing, our protection. He is our glorification. Nothing of Him happens to us except as we are properly related in Him.

He is in us and we are in Him, just as He is in the Father and the Father is in Him. We are one with Him (John 17:21).

When He told His disciples that He was going to prepare a place for them, He was talking about a place in Father. *"In My Father's house are many mansions,"* or abodes, dwellings (John 14:2). John 17:3 explains that eternal life is knowing God and Jesus Christ whom God had sent.

Jesus explained in John 15:1ff that He is the true vine. We are to abide in Him (v. 4). Without Him we can do nothing (v. 5).

If we abide in Him and His words abide in us, we will ask what we desire and it shall be done for us. What do we ask for? That we should bear much fruit for Him and so be His disciple. By this Father God is glorified (vv. 7-8).

This is a mystery, but one that must be understood and, moreover, one that must become a reality in every believer. We cannot abide both in the world and in heaven at the same time. We cannot abide in the flesh and Spirit at the same time. We cannot abide in sin and righteousness at the same time. We cannot abide in Satan and Christ at the same time.

We are going to bring glory to something or someone. We are going to seek to glorify ourselves, another man, or by our evil deeds bring glory to Satan and his works of darkness.

We will constantly fellowship in something. We will fellowship either in the Word or the world. You can't have it both ways.

God is so dealing with His holy ones today so as to bring them to the end of self into a holy and pure, undefiled relationship with Him—not for us (though it ends up being for us), but for Him, that He might be all in all.

We are going from faith to faith (Rom. 1:17), from glory to glory (2 Cor. 3:18). It is a process God is dealing in us. We are being conformed into His image (Rom. 8:29) and being transformed by the renewing of our minds that we might prove what is that good and acceptable and perfect will of God (Rom. 12:2).

Any righteousness we think we have is not, nor ever could be, of our own. It is His righteousness. He is righteous. Get into Him!

Any sanctification we think we have is not, nor ever could be, of our own. It is His holiness. He alone is holy. Get into Him!

Any glorification we think we have is not, nor ever could be, of our own. It is His glory! He alone is worthy. Get into Him!

Jesus Prayed Us through to Glory

There's a great little chorus we sing, "From glory to glory, He's changing me, changing me, changing me; His likeness and image to perfect in me—the love of God shown to the world."

We find that His great salvation is all wrapped up in who He is, not in who we are; in what He has done, not in what we could ever in a thousand lifetimes hope to do.

"For by grace are you saved through faith; and that not of yourselves: it is the gift of God: not of works, lest any man should boast. For we are His workmanship, created in Christ Jesus unto good works, which God has before ordained that we should walk in them" (Eph. 2:8-10).

Jesus' priestly prayer in John 17 includes this progression from Passover to Pentecost to Tabernacles; that is, from justification to sanctification to glorification.

JUSTIFICATION/REDEMPTION. *"Father, the hour is come, glorify Your Son, that Your Son also may glorify You, as You have given Him power over all flesh, that he should give eternal life to as many as you have given him"* (John 17:1b-2 NKJV).

Jesus was looking toward the hour of His own glorification when He prayed this prayer. Through His death, burial, resurrection, and ascension He would be returning to the glory He had with Father before the world was (v. 5).

Furthermore, He was already glorified in the disciples who believed in Him and became His through faith (v. 10).

So, in the glory of His death, burial, and resurrection, He gave eternal life: justification and redemption.

SANCTIFICATION. But He was leaving the world and was leaving them in the world. So as He continued in prayer, He asked that Father-God keep them through His name that they might be one as He and the Father are one (John 17:11).

"Sanctify them through your truth. Your word is truth" (v. 17). As Father sent Him into the world, He is sending them into the world (v. 18). He sanctified Himself for their sakes that they may be sanctified by the truth. Thus, He sent the Holy Spirit, the administrator of truth, to sanctify them with the truth.

Jesus explained to His disciples that it was to their advantage for Him to go away so He could send the Helper (the Paraclete: one who goes alongside of), the Holy Spirit (John 16:7). When the Spirit of truth comes, He will guide them into all truth (v. 13). Sanctification is a guiding, progressive process.

GLORIFICATION. So the Holy Spirit is given not only to continue to glorify the pattern Son, Jesus, but that God might bring many sons to glory (Heb. 2:10).

Jesus prayed, *"And the glory which you gave me I have*

given them; that they may be one, even as We are one: I in them and You in Me: that they may be made perfect in one..." (John 17:22-23).

"That they may be made perfect..." relates again to the continuing work of sanctification intended to bring us to the finished work of glorification.

And we have it again and again—three feasts, three courts, three phases in our walk with the Lord. *"Be therefore perfect, even as your Father which is in heaven is perfect"!* (Matt. 5:48). The word "perfect" means mature, complete.

Do you hunger to go on with Him? Are you willing to be baptized in the Holy Spirit and fire in order to bring that ultimate glory to God in Christ Jesus?

Let us not fall short of the glory of God (Rom. 3:23).

Chapter 8

As He Is

In 1 Corinthians 2:1-2, the apostle Paul explains that he had not come to them with superior speech or wisdom; that is, with great philosophical platitudes, theological treatises, or religious jargon. He determined to know nothing more when he was among them except Jesus Christ and Him crucified. For in that person, Jesus, and His death upon a Roman cross was not only contained all the purposes of God but the fulfillment of those purposes. What more was there to know?

Many Sons to Glory

Not only were God's eternal purposes fulfilled in Jesus Christ crucified, but Jesus set in motion an adoption program whereby God as Father would birth for Himself many sons to glory just as He, Jesus, was the Son of glory. Whatever was fulfilled in Jesus was predetermined to be fulfilled in the many sons as well.

Jesus was Himself justified by the very life He lived and, thereby, became the justifier of all who believe in Him. Through faith in Him who justified, the believer becomes as He was—justified.

In this same vein, He was the righteousness of God. In Him we are made the righteousness of God. *"For He [God] has made Him to be sin for us, who knew no sin; that we might be made the righteousness of God in Him"* (2 Cor. 5:21). *"Who His own self bore our sins in His own body on the tree, that we, being dead to sins, should live unto righteousness: by whose stripes you were healed [saved, made whole]"* (1 Peter 2:24).

Whatever He was and is, He is that for us. He is our redeemer and our redemption. He is our justifier and our justification. He is our savior and our salvation. He is our
sanctifier and our sanctification. He is our glorifier and
our glorification.

The revelation of who Jesus is comes to us in demon-
stration of the Spirit and of power (1 Cor. 2:4ff). For *"God
has revealed them unto us by His Spirit: for the Spirit
searches all things, even the deep things of God"* (v. 10).
This is why we've been given the Spirit—why we have to go
on to Pentecost, into the Holy Place—so that we might
know by the Spirit the things freely given to us by God (v.
12).

What has God freely given to us? His justification, His
sanctification, His glorification; that is, His salvation.
How did He do that? By giving us Himself in the form of
human flesh, made like a man yet without sin. He gave us
Jesus Christ crucified. And when we received Him through
faith, we became what He is.

Now this is powerful stuff—the kind of stuff that can
only be revealed in the power of the Spirit. It is not a wisdom of this age nor of the rulers of this age; that is, of natural, temporal sources. It is that wisdom that comes from
God by having the mind of Christ. *"For who has known
the mind of the Lord, that he may instruct Him? But we
have the mind of Christ"* (v. 16).

What are you going to instruct God? What could you
possibly instruct God, you who are mere creatures of God?
If we have the mind of Christ, we have that wisdom that is
not of this world. We have godly wisdom. We know who
God is and what God wants. We instruct Him according to
His word and His will.

What is the model prayer Jesus taught His disciples?
He told them to pray "Our Father...." From this beginning
they were instructed to approach the throne of God boldly
and make their request. Their every request was in keeping with God's word, will, and eternal purposes. Yet, they
were to instruct Him through prayer to answer their
prayer—the very thing God wants to do.

I am finding that we get our best and most out of God

when we make a demand upon Him to impart Himself to us. God desperately wants to impart all that was given by Jesus at the cross. But He will never impose Himself upon us. He always positions Himself so we might seek after Him. He is always approachable, always accessible, always present, never allowing us to suffer the lack of Him beyond our ability (1 Cor. 10:13), but He is not cheap.

He cannot be purchased, but He is not cheap. It cost Jesus everything which He freely laid down for our sakes. *"Let this mind be in you, which was also in Christ Jesus: who, being in the form of God, thought it not robbery to be equal with God: but made Himself of no reputation, and took upon Him the form of a servant, and was made in the likeness of men: and being found in fashion as a man, He humbled himself, and became obedient unto death, even the death of the cross"* (Phil. 2:5-8).

The Abandonment of Self

For His believers to attain Him, though He is freely given, they must, as He did, abandon themselves in pursuit of God. We have preached a cheap believism gospel that has deceived multitudes. Only by the grace and mercy of God will they enter into His glory.

But "this gospel of the kingdom" which calls for our participation into His death (Rom. 6:3-11) and a sharing in His suffering (Phil. 3:10) is being restored by the Spirit of God today to those who have ears to hear and eyes to see.

The irony of the gospel is this: that the only way one can come into the things of God—that is, into God—is through the willful laying down of his own life, to follow Jesus in His baptism. He was baptized in water which was the sign at the beginning of His ministry that pointed to the spiritual baptism of His death and burial.

"Are you able...to be baptized with the baptism that I am baptized with...?" He poignantly asked His disciples. They answered, *"We are able."* Then he promised their baptism in His suffering by saying, *"You shall drink indeed of My cup, and be baptized with the baptism that I am baptized with"* (Matt. 20:22-23).

Jesus returned to glory through the path of death, resurrection, and ascension. He had to go to and through the cross. Those who wish to go to glory with Him, to share in His glory, must themselves take up their cross daily and follow Him (Luke 9:23). This is the abandonment of self.

To Become like Jesus

"But we speak the wisdom of God in a mystery, even the hidden wisdom, which God ordained before the world unto our glory: which none of the princes of this world knew: for had they known it, they would not have crucified the Lord of glory" (1 Cor. 2:7-8).

There is a predestined glory awaiting the sons of God that is likened unto the glory of the Son of God. Had the rulers of this age been able to understand this mystery, this irony of the cross, they would never have crucified the Lord of glory .

Now generally the rulers of this age are thought of in Scripture as being demonic forces (Eph 6:12). Satan himself is described as the prince of the power of the air (Eph. 2:2). Jesus destroyed all the works of the devil (1 John 3:8).

So it stands to reason that what Paul means in 1 Corinthians 2:8 is that Satan would never have carried out the death of Jesus had he known that His death would mean His glorification. Satan moved upon covetous and power-hungry men to crucify the Lord of glory and in the process destroyed his own works—another irony of the gospel.

"But as it is written," Paul quotes from Isaiah 64:4, things were happening that *"Eye has not seen nor ear heard, neither have entered into the heart of man, the things which God has prepared for them that love him"* (1 Cor. 2:9).

This verse has been tossed about like pearls cast to the swine by those who want to use it to claim material possessions for themselves. *"For what shall it profit a man, if he shall gain the whole world, and lose his own soul?"* (Mark 8:36).

Let me ask you—and beware! Your answer will give you away. If you could make this verse to mean for you that you could either gain the world or attain to all of who Christ is, which would you choose? Would you still choose

Him at all cost to self, to life, to material gain? What, after all, was the problem with the young ruler who wanted eternal life (Luke 18:18ff)? The scripture says he went away sorrowful because he had much riches.

Can a rich man get to heaven? Certainly! As long as his riches aren't his god; as long as he does not put his trust in them to the extent they rule him; as long as he could give them up for the sake of the gospel.

Ah! There is so much more here than anything in this old world could ever offer in a million lifetimes: to become like Jesus! To be revealed before the whole world as a glorified son of God. Not that we seek the glory for self, but for the glory of God that we might truly be to the praise of His glory (Eph. 1:6,12).

Now here's what we're coming to: what has God prepared for those who love Him? Healthy bodies? Cadillacs? Come on. Look at Him closer. What does God want? Read 1 Corinthians 2:7 again, *"But we speak the wisdom of God in a mystery, even the hidden wisdom, which God ordained before the world unto our glory."*

What God wants in us is the very same as He had in Jesus. Jesus was the pattern, the blueprint, the temple, the head of the body. Follow Him through His life, death, burial, resurrection, and ascension.

We are being manifested (brought forth, made visible, revealed) as sons just as He was the Son. Now we are not gods. Don't run off with this. Don't get arrogant. Remember, the only way that anyone can get into the Kingdom of God is on bent knees.

The devil's counterfeit to this end-time manifestation of sonship is in the New Age movement whereby arrogant men think that they are gods and that they can perfect themselves and their world by getting in harmony with one another and creation by means of meditation and all other demonic occult practices.

How can the created ones ever expect to be in harmony with anything apart from their Creator? It is foolishness that is leading straight to the pits of hell.

But where there is a counterfeit, there must be a reality. There is a glory that awaits the true sons of God.

To Become What Jesus Was

The glory of the sons is that they take on the nature of the Son. This is radical and hard to say, but it translates thus:

As He was the righteousness of God, in Him we become the righteousness of God. As He was perfect without sin, we become perfect without sin in this life. *"Be ye therefore perfect, even as your Father which is in heaven is perfect"* (Matt. 5:48). Would God ask of us something impossible? With men it is impossible, in the flesh it is impossible, but with God all things are possible (Matt. 19:26; Mark 10:27; Luke 18:27).

Jesus was justified before God, thereby became our justification, thereby our justifier, thereby we are justified just as He was.

Jesus was sanctified before God, thereby became our sanctification, thereby our sanctifier, thereby we are sanctified just as He was. (We are sanctified by the blood [Heb. 13:12], the word [John 17:17], and the Spirit [1 Cor. 6:11]).

Jesus was glorified (John 13:31; Acts 3:13) before God, thereby became our glorification, thereby our glorifier (Rom. 8:30), thereby, we are glorified (Rom. 8:17) just as He was.

The strength of what I'm trying to say is in the phrase "just as He was." Scripture bears me out. John, writing about Him in the context of love, said, *"Beloved, now are we the sons of God, and it does not yet appear what we shall be: but we know that, when He shall appear, we shall be like Him; for we shall see Him as He is"* (1 John 3:2).

Jesus is manifesting Himself—that is, revealing Himself—more and more even before He comes in all of His glory. Those to whom He reveals Himself are themselves being changed into His nature.

When Moses came down from the mountain after being in the presence of God for forty days, He not only shone forth the glory on his face but had the word of God within him. He had that Law within Him. He knew the heart of God and felt what God felt. That's why he threw the tablets of stone down when he saw harlot Israel dancing orgies around their golden calf.

The more you are in the presence of God, the more you will become as He is.

You are becoming whatever you fellowship in—whether in sin and the world or in righteousness and heavenly things. *"Bad company corrupts good morals"* (1 Cor. 15:33 NAS).

To Become the Word

In the past we've tried to attain to the things of God by appropriating the word of God. We've tried to get healed, delivered, and blessed by confessing the word. We talked about getting the word down into our spirits.

The reality of it all is that nothing can be attained by trying to appropriate the word. We are going to have to become the word. Jesus was the Word made flesh. As we are in Him and He in us, we too become as He is, the Word of God. As He was the Word made flesh, we who are flesh are being made the word.

As He is love, we are love; as He is peace, we are peace; as He is joy, we are joy; as He is patience, goodness, kindness, et al., so are we.

As He is the Spirit, so are we of the Spirit. The gifts of the Holy Spirit are simply the impartation of the Spirit Himself. When we operate in the word of knowledge, this is not a thing we have, but the person of the Spirit which comes from being in relationship with Him.

We don't just have a gift from the Spirit, we are given the Spirit and thereby become one with Him. We are either one with Him or not. The Bible says we're one. It's like mixing water with water. When His Spirit causes our human spirits to be reborn after His very nature, we have Spirit mixed with Spirit; not our spirit, but His.

On Becoming God's Instrument of Himself

Jesus said, *"If you abide in Me, and My words abide in you, you shall ask what you will, and it shall be done unto you"* (John 15:7). If you ask for anything for self, you only show that you're not really abiding in the word. If you abide in Him and His word abides in you, you not only want what He wants, but you become the means through which He gets it.

God wanted people healed. So He sent Jesus to heal. Jesus never prayed for anyone to be healed. He healed them. He then commissioned us to go and do likewise—lay hands on the sick and heal them.

God did not want people possessed and oppressed with demons, so He sent Jesus, the deliverer, to set the captives free. Jesus didn't pray for them to be set free. He cast the devils out. He then gave His disciples authority to tread upon serpents and scorpions and over all the power of the enemy with the assurance that nothing by any means should harm them (Luke 10:19).

God did not want any man to perish, so He sent His only begotten Son that whoever believed in Him should not perish but have everlasting life (John 3:16). Jesus doesn't pray for people's salvation. He shed His blood and thereby forgave them of their sins and saved them.

He then commissioned His disciples to go, teach, baptize (Matt. 28:18-20). We are to certainly pray for people's salvation. But too often that's as far as we go. We have even been given authority to forgive sins: *"Whose soever sins you remit, they are remitted unto them; and whose soever sins you retain, they are retained"* (John 20:23).

This authority to forgive sins offends our minds, but consider further the strength of a preceding statement in verse 21: *"As My Father has sent Me, so send I you."* The Father sent Jesus bearing the same life of which He, the Father, was. In the power and authority of that life, Jesus not only acted on behalf of God, but was God. It was God's life. Throughout his gospel, John pounds in the idea that whoever believes in Jesus has this life within them also. Now think about that!

We are not nor ever could be the Savior. Jesus alone is Savior. We had best give up trying to save people in our own strength. No one can ever be saved by the shedding of our blood any more than by the blood of goats and sheep and bulls (Heb. 10:4). Jesus alone is the Savior. We are atoned only by His precious, righteous, holy, undefiled blood. Praise His holy name.

Nevertheless, we are His witnesses. The message of evangelism today is that the winning of souls cannot and will not be achieved through programs, printed tracts, campaigns, etc., but at the hands of those who dare to become as He is: living epistles—His life let loose in the world.

As He lives and moves in and through us, molding us after His nature, filling us with His Spirit, pouring us out with His life, then and only then will the world see, come to know, and be won over to the King of kings and Lord of lords.

"...As He is, so are we in this world" (1 John 4:17).

What things has eye not seen, nor ear heard, nor yet entered the heart of man? The revelation of the glorified Jesus and the revealing of His crucified ones—bearing His image to glory.

Chapter 9

Entering His Rest

The emergence of the crucified ones is, at the same time, the abolition of dead works. All that is accomplished through them will be accomplished in rest.

"There remains therefore a rest to the people of God" (Heb. 4:9).

The writer of Hebrews was concerned that his readers might follow in the way of their fathers (Israel) who died in the wilderness and did not enter into their promised rest because of their unbelief (Heb. 3:16-19).

But God had promised a rest for His people. God cannot go back on His word. So, if they failed to enter in, He has reserved a people who will enter into His rest, who will fulfill His promise. *"There remains therefore a rest to the people of God."*

What is this rest and how do we come into it? No doubt we all feel the wearisomeness of our works. More often than not we feel like our works are dead. The only way we can keep them going is to keep them going. That which is of God does not have to be kept going by our strength. We have no ability whatsoever to produce anything worthy for God by our own power. *"Not by might, not by power, but by My Spirit, says the Lord of hosts"* (Zech. 4:6).

Faith and Rest

The possibility existed that these believers in Christ Jesus might also depart from the living God through unbelief which the writer says reflects an evil heart (Heb. 3:12).

"For we," he says, *"are made partakers of Christ if we*

hold the beginning of our confidence steadfast to the end" (Heb. 3:14).

This threat is so real in the opinion of the writer of Hebrews that he charges them to fear lest any of them seem to come short of entering this rest (Heb. 4:1).

We see here the relationship between rest and faith. The fact is that the "rest" of God is the direct result of having faith in God. For one who is out of rest is out of faith. When one is in faith—that is, resting in the finished work of God—he is in his best position to please God. For without faith it is impossible to please God (Heb. 11:6).

The good news of God was preached to us, the writer of Hebrews explains, as well as to them, referring back to their Israelite fathers in the wilderness. They had the witness of God given to them through Moses. But the word they heard didn't profit them, didn't bring them into their promised rest, because they did not mix what they heard with faith (Heb. 4:2). For we who believe enter that rest.

A lot of people say they believe, but they are not in rest. They say they believe that God is on the throne, but they do not live their lives accordingly. They live in fear, worry, anxiety, discouragement, and the like. They struggle to make a way for themselves as though they can order their own steps. They pull, tug, agonize to manipulate their circumstances until those circumstances agree with their plan. They lie, cheat, steal—do whatever—to try to get ahead. But all of those things are the deeds of unbelief. As though God is not able!

Faith and God's Finished Work

The writer of Hebrews wanted his audience and us today to have faith in the work of God which was finished from the foundation of the world (Heb. 4:3b). If God has rested from His works, what are we in such a stew about?

Once in the past, I was trying desperately in my own strength to do something for God. We all want to. And the Spirit of the Lord witnessed to me, "When you work, I rest. When you rest, I work."

When we enter into faith, knowing that God knows the end from the beginning, that *"we are His workmanship created in Christ Jesus to good works which God has ordained that we should walk in them"* (Eph. 2:10) and that *"all things work together for good to them that love God, to them who are the called according to His purpose"* (Rom. 8:28), then we obey the Master's voice, *"Take no thought (do not be anxious) for your life..."* (Matt. 6:25-34).

Mark 11:22 says, *"Have faith in God."* Many people have taken that to mean that we are to have faith in God for things—for whatever we want. This stress on faith for things has been so overworked that some are trying to have faith in faith.

There is a receiving from God that results from our participation in God. For as we come more and more to know Him, we will know His heart, His will, His ways, and will ask for that.

But the emphasis, I believe, in Mark 11:22-24 is "in God." Have faith in God. Period. Have faith in His finished works. Believe the word of God, for the word of God is the will of God. The word of God is the expression of His heart. The word of God is God expressed in words. His word must be fulfilled. It will be the completing, summing up of all things into Him (Eph. 1:10).

Faith and Dead Works

The faith we are to have that brings us into that promised rest is not easily attained. *"Let us labor therefore to enter that rest, lest any man fall after the same example of unbelief"* (Heb. 4:11).

The fact is, our flesh-man nature is fallen and still under the curse of works. We cannot imagine a gospel that does not require some works on our part. We have to labor to stay in faith and rest.

Most of the thrust of institutional Christianity is based on works. Believers are made to feel guilty if they do not perform according to the rules, regulations, doctrines, traditions, and many unwritten expectations put upon them by those who want to control and own them. They are under the letter of the law in their own churches and have had the Spirit of life suppressed in them.

Jesus, Our Sabbath Rest

But there is coming forth a people who are looking toward Tabernacles, who are entering the Holy of Holies—entering that place of absolute faith in God—entering that promised rest.

They are no longer interested in works for works' sake. They have no agenda of their own that they want to promote. They have nothing of self to gain. Their whole preoccupation is to seek the will of God and do it.

When we diligently obey the word of the Lord, we will find that He, the Spirit of truth, the Comforter, will always bring us into rest. He will bring us into Jesus who has become for us our Sabbath rest.

More than anything else, Jesus wanted to make the point that He was the fulfillment of God's Sabbath. He was the fulfillment of all the Law and the prophets. Everything the prophets said about God was completed in Jesus who was God.

The classic example of this statement is found in Matthew 12:1-8. Jesus and His disciples went through a grain field and, being hungry, ate of it. The Pharisees saw them and asked Jesus why they were doing what was unlawful to do on the Sabbath. He answered by declaring that He, the Son of Man, is Lord even of the Sabbath day.

Jesus is the Sabbath rest for all who believe in Him, for all who put their trust in Him, who put their trust in the fact that on the cross He finished the work of God.

There remain those in Christendom who still debate whether we should go to church and worship God on Saturday, being the Sabbath, or on Sunday, the day of His resurrection.

They fail to recognize, first of all, that the church is the people of God and not a place to go and, secondly, that God is not seeking Saturday or Sunday worshipers only. *"The hour comes, and now is, when the true worshipers shall worship the Father in spirit and in truth; for the Father seeks such to worship Him. God is a Spirit* [not law]: *and they that worship Him must worship Him in spirit and in truth* [not in legalism]*"* (John 4:23-24).

We are the temple of the Holy Spirit. We are living and

moving shrines in which God Almighty has taken up residence that we might be a chosen generation, a royal priesthood, a holy nation, His own peculiar people—that we might show forth His praises who has called us out of darkness into His marvelous light (1 Pet. 2:9).

When God gave Moses instruction for the observance of the Sabbath day and of the annual feasts, he repeatedly called them into rest. He commanded them six separate times throughout Leviticus 23, *"You shall do no servile work..."* Servile suggests the submissive behavior characteristic of a slave. The term had a religious usage. It spoke of the service or worship of God.

The Old Testament is the type in the natural realm of that which became spiritual reality in the New Testament. Jesus has become for us our Sabbath rest, and we enter into that rest by being in Him every day of every week.

Faith and Obedience

Now as never before, if we ever hope to be in the company of the crucified ones, we will have to enter into that Sabbath rest.

We enter that rest by radical obedience to the Spirit of God. To radically obey is to radically believe and trust in God to the point of appearing foolish to the world.

Joshua was given the tremendous task of taking the stronghold of Jericho. There was no way in human strength or ingenuity that he could have done this. But God made a ridiculous demand upon him.

God told him before he went up against Jericho that He had given Jericho into his hands (Josh. 6:2). Joshua had the word of God before he had the reality of it in the natural realm. But that's all he needed. He knew God. He had relationship with this God. He knew that God's word was His promise, that it was a sure thing.

For six days he was to march around the city one time. The priests were to bear the seven trumpets of rams' horns and go out in front of the ark of the covenant. The ark of the covenant was the presence of God. Where God is, there is the power of God.

Then on the seventh day, they were to march around

the city seven times and the priests were to blow the trumpets. When the people heard the long blast of the trumpet, the walls would come tumbling down.

Now they definitely had something to do, and some may have grown weary walking and waiting seven days; but, compared to the task at hand, they took the city in rest. God did all the work. They were to simply obey.

Throughout the scriptures, time after time, we see the power of God released through obedience. Obedience, faith, and rest are merely synonyms—different ways of saying the same thing.

There will always be directives for us to obey, but they will always be given in grace and with the anointing of the Spirit. What God appoints, He anoints.

If we find ourselves "slaving," doing servile work in spiritual matters, we are going to meet the displeasure of our God. At one point, God warned that any person caught doing work on the Day of Atonement would be destroyed (Lev. 23:30). Why? Because Jesus atoned for the sins of the world. We can't work to earn our atonement (or salvation).

"For by grace are you saved through faith..." (Eph. 2:8). We can never get away from this passage. I call it the plumb line of the gospel. If any man adds anything to it or tries to take anything away from it, He is of the circumcision party—a modern day Judaizer.

In Leviticus 23, The New King James Version of the Bible translates "servile" as "customary." *"You shall do no customary work..."* I favor the way the New American Standard has rendered it: *"You shall do no laborious work..."*

If any person in Christ has more to do than he has time to do, some of those things are not of the Lord. He is in unrest and out of faith. He is into dead works—wood, hay, and stubble to be cast into the fire and burned.

The only enduring works of gold and silver are brought forth through the refiner's fire of obedience. God is at work, bringing to reality that which has already been finished.

"Let us labor therefore to enter into that rest..." (Heb. 4:11).

Obey Him explicitly in every way.

Live the crucified life that the glory of the Lord might be revealed in and through you in this final hour before He comes.

Chapter 10

Old Order/New Order:
The Is-ness of God in Us

The crucified ones are a new breed of Christians in the world today. They are new order in contrast to an old order of Christians.

The old order of Christians are essentially under law—not necessarily the law of the Old Testament, but laws of their own making. They are kept by rules and regulations that govern them because they are not governed and motivated by the power and life of God working within them.

Giving

Under the old order, the Christian has to be prompted to give. Under the new order, the Christian is by nature a giver. The old is under the law to tithe. The new is the tithe; that is, all that he is and has is an offering of first fruits unto his God.

Everything he is and has is God's upon demand. He does not have to be exhorted by the preacher to do or give anything. He is one step in front of the preacher. He is constantly in tune with the Holy Spirit who is leading him in everything he does, says, or gives.

Faithfulness

Under the old order, the Christian has to be exhorted to faithfulness. Under the new, he is by nature faithful. He comes and goes and does according to his Father's will.

He is faithful because he is trusting. He believes in God and puts his trust in God and has confidence in God that *"all things work together for good to them who love God, to them who are the called according to His purpose"* (Rom. 8:28).

Because he trusts in God, he, himself, is trustworthy. I have found over the years that he who cannot trust others cannot himself be trusted. We tend to project upon others what we see in ourselves.

Trusting persons are faithful persons. Faithful persons are obedient persons. It's not that they are faithful and obedient to do what they are told; they are faithful and obedient to be what they have been made to be. In other words, faithfulness and obedience comes out of who they are. They have been shaped and reshaped by their Maker to be as He is.

Churching

Now this very important distinction between old order Christian and new order Christian is going to become more evident with time.

The old order Christian goes to church. He has to be programmed to go, exhorted to faithfulness in attendance, encouraged in program participation, etc. The church is what he does. In most cases, church is his religion.

But the new order Christian is the church. He sees himself as the very extension of Jesus Christ in the world today. He does not have to be exhorted to go to church, he is the temple of the Holy Spirit together with all other true believers.

In this new order, among this new breed, is a sense of tiredness from playing church. They are not interested in churchianity any more. They are released in the world to be the church.

They understand very well that the body must gather from time to time to gain strength from one another through the ministries, gifts, and fruit of the Spirit placed in the body. They gather for strength and scatter for service.

Praying

The old order Christian has to be exhorted to pray while the new order Christian is the prayer. That is, he is in such constant communion with the Father through the Spirit that he knows the mind of Christ and has taken on the image of his Father through Christ. He does not have to "pray" for answers so much as he is the answer to prayer.

He doesn't necessarily pray for someone's healing. He heals him in Jesus' name when he sees by the Spirit that healing is what Father is doing. He, like his big brother Jesus before him, does only what he sees his Father doing.

He is a walking prayer meeting.

Fasting

He may fast often. But his greatest fast is not in the denial of certain food and drink from time to time, but in the total denial of his self-life at all times. Therefore, he is a living fast unto his God.

Praising

He does not have to be exhorted to praise as do old order Christians. He is to the praise of his Father. Praise wells up from within him as rivers of living water. He praises all the day long. Praise is forever on his lips. He can't help but praise because praise for his God is the abundance of his heart.

Worshiping

Likewise, worship! He does not have to have a bulletin to guide him in his worship. He does not have to go to this mountain or that (to this cathedral or that) on his appointed high days before he can worship. Neither is Father seeking this form of worship.

For the hour comes and now is that the Father is seeking a people who will worship Him in spirit and truth (John 4:23).

You cannot worship Him in truth except in spirit. He is both Spirit and Truth. The true worshiper, therefore, must worship Him while abiding in Him.

Doing Good

The old order Christian has to be exhorted to do good. He has to have laws, creeds, doctrines, rules and regulations spelled out for him so he can know how to live righteously. But this is law. The letter kills.

The Spirit of God who abides within the new order Christian is Himself the administrator of the law written within the heart of the believer.

This new order Christian is the righteousness of God.

"Who [Jesus] His own self bore our sins in His own body on the tree: that we, being dead to sins, should live unto righteousness: by whose stripes you were healed [saved, made whole]" (1 Pet. 2:24).

"For He [God] has made Him [Jesus] to be sin for us, who knew no sin: that we might be made the righteousness of God in Him" (2 Cor. 5:21).

The doing of good for the new order Christian is irrelevant, for the goodness of God is manifested through him.

Doing/Being

And so it goes with everything else that can be said of the Christian life. The old order is an outward order of doing, while the new order is the inward reality of being.

Of course, it holds true that whatever one is on the inside will determine what he does on the outside. The difference between being religious and being born again is this—that one who is born again has his very nature changed by the power of God. Religion, at best, can only control or modify the outward behavior of a person.

He who is born again was once one thing; now he is another. *"Therefore if any man is in Christ, he is a new creature: old things are passed away; behold, all things are become new"* (2 Cor. 5:17).

Godliness

The old man of flesh has been crucified and buried in the very death and burial of Jesus Christ. He is history so far as God is concerned. Only the devil and the flesh itself are interested in keeping that old man of flesh alive.

The old order Christian tries at best to mimic godliness, to imitate Christ. The new order Christian has the very nature of godliness birthed in him and is thus becoming more godly day by day. As God is—so is he!

The Is-ness of God

When God called Moses to go to Egypt and lead the Israelites out of their bondage, Moses wanted to know what he should tell them when they asked the name of the God of their fathers. God answered, *"I AM THAT I AM"* (Ex. 3:13-14). This is related to the name YHWH, or Yahweh (transliterated Jehovah), which is derived from the verb *hayah*, "to be." The verb of being! God does not stand in history with a past and a future. He is forever present. He is!

For this reason, Jesus, being God, is *"the same yester-day, and today, and forever"* (Heb. 13:8).

God invented time. He is the author of history. He already knows the end from the beginning. He has determined it. Yet, in His sovereignty and omnipotence, He is able to allow the freedom of human wills. (His ways are not our ways... Is. 55:8.)

It helps us in our faith to understand the "is-ness" of God.

Bearing His Nature

But it goes beyond this.

Jesus made it clear that He was the "I AM" of the Old Testament (John 8:58). Throughout John's gospel the Greek words *ego eimi*, which literally translates "I, I am," was used to explain Jesus. Using this term, He said of Himself:

I AM
> Messiah (John 4:25-26)
> the Bread of Life (John 6:35,48,51)
> the Light of the World (John 8:12)
> the Door of the Sheep (John 10:7)
> the Good Shepherd (John 10:11)
> the Resurrection and the Life (John 11:25)
> Master (Teacher) and Lord (John 13:13)
> the Way, the Truth, and the Life (John 14:6)
> the True Vine (John 15:1)
> Jesus (which means Salvation) (John 18:5-8)

"...as He is so are we in this world" (1 John 4:17).
He is love, so we are love.
He is righteous, so we are righteous.
He is faith, so we are faith.
He is spirit, so we are spirit.
He is truth, so we are truth.
He is eternal life, so we are eternal life.
He is! So, we are!

As He is the great I AM, we have become in Him little "I am's."

Jesus said of Himself, *"I am the Light of the world"* (John 8:12). He said to His disciples, *"You are the light of the world"* (Matt. 5:14). The only way his disciples can be light is to have the Light of Life living within them and shining through them. There is no way you can imitate Him. You are either of His very nature or you are a phony.

This is not an ego trip for us to embark upon. I must remind the reader that we enter in through repentance: meekness, gentleness, humility, submissiveness, faithfulness, obedience. We take on His nature—He who emptied Himself.

The new order Christian, this new breed of crucified ones are becoming more and more like Him. It is less a matter of doing and more a matter of being.

Jesus did what He did because of who He was. So it is with us who go on from glory to glory, faith to faith—we will do more out of who we are than out of any religious expectations put upon us.

Chapter 11

Water into Wine

The bringing forth of the crucified ones is the new thing God is doing in the world today. They are the new wine being poured into new wineskins.

When Jesus performed the miracle at Cana (John 2), He changed the water into wine. Water in the Bible is generally a type of the word of God (Eph. 5:26), and wine represents the blood of Jesus as He spoke of Himself regarding the Lord's supper. *"Likewise also the cup after supper, saying, 'This cup is the new testament in My blood, which is shed for you'"* (Luke 22:20).

It isn't until the water of the word of God becomes the wine of the blood of God that it has any redemptive value. Jesus was the Word made flesh (John 1:1,14). He was also the Lamb of God (John 1:36; Rev. 5:5-10). He came as the Word and died as the Lamb. The Word became the Blood: the water became wine.

Prophetic Nature of the Event

I believe that John is making a deliberate statement by the Holy Spirit in preserving this miracle at Cana as the *"beginning of miracles Jesus did in Cana of Galilee, and manifested forth His glory..."* (John 2:11). It serves prophetically of both the crucifixion of Jesus and of the emergence of the crucified ones in these last times.

The fact that this was in the context of a wedding is significant. The whole story of the Bible begins and ends with a wedding. In the beginning He made man, and from him He made a helpmate and declared that *"they shall be one flesh"* (Gen. 2:24).

Ephesians 5:22-33 draws the correlation between the husband and wife, and Christ and the church. God and Christ are viewed throughout the Bible as the husband or bridegroom while Israel and the church are viewed as His wife or bride. Israel and the church are one and the same from God's point of view. He has always and only had one bride in His eye. He did not divorce one and remarry another. He divorced Himself from the harlot Israel (Jer. 3:8) but promised her restoration in Zion (Jer. 3:14-19).

John the Baptist was quoted as saying in reference to Jesus, *"He who has the bride is the bridegroom"* (John 3:29).

Jesus Himself compared His coming again to a wedding feast involving five wise and five foolish virgins (Matt. 25:1-13).

Revelation 19:7-9 pictures this end-of-the-age wedding thus, *"Let us be glad and rejoice, and give honor to Him: for the marriage of the Lamb is come, and His wife has made herself ready. And to her was granted that she should be arrayed in fine linen, clean and white: for the fine linen is the righteousness of saints...Blessed are they who are called to the marriage supper of the Lamb..."*

It appears significant that the wedding at Cana took place on the third day after Jesus had been baptized by John in the river Jordan which marked the beginning of His ministry. The number three in the Bible speaks of the fullness of testimony. The third day, therefore, possibly alludes to Christ as He was manifested in the glory of His resurrection (Acts 10:40, Luke 13:32).

In this same way, the emergence of these crucified ones in this final hour is the expected manifestation (revealing) of the sons of God spoken of in Romans 8:18-19. *"For I reckon that the sufferings of this present time are not worthy to be compared with the glory which shall be revealed in us. For the earnest expectation of the creature waits for the manifestation (revelation) of the sons of God."*

Furthermore, I think it is significant that the mother of Jesus was there both to instruct the son and the servants. The Church universal has always been regarded as a mother figure. In Revelation 12 we are told of the man child who is to be birthed out of great travail from the woman. This man child is first a picture of Christ Himself, but also a picture of this many-membered Christ-man who is to be manifested as many sons (male and female alike) in this last hour.

Radical Obedience

"And when they wanted wine, the mother of Jesus said to Him, 'They have no wine.' Jesus said to her, 'Woman, what have I to do with you? My hour is not yet come'" (John 2:3-4).

Jesus clearly was not referring to His hour to do miracles because He promptly performed one. He was instead referring to the hour of His appointed crucifixion. In so doing, He tied this wedding and wine event to the shedding of His precious blood on the cross.

Mary, knowing full well who this Son of hers was and perhaps having a word of knowledge that He was about to perform this miracle, turned to the servants and instructed them to do whatever He said to them (v. 5). The servants not only must have known who Mary was but also respected her authority in this situation.

Now the servants, I believe, symbolically represent ministry; more specifically, of the equipping gift ministries of Ephesians 4:11. (Scripturally speaking, every believer ought to view himself as a servant, even though we are children, sons, priests, etc.)

The Greek word used here in John 2 for servants is *diakonoi*. This is the word from which we get the English word "deacon" in the English. It has often been translated "minister" in the New Testament. It primarily speaks of one who is doing the work of a servant.

The equipping gift ministries of Ephesians 4:11 have a particular anointing from the Holy Spirit to preach and teach the word of God. They are given charge over the word. In the early days of the church, the apostles charged the congregation to appoint deacons *(diakonoi)* to look after the temporal affairs of the body in order that they might give themselves continually to prayer and to the ministry *(diakonia)* of the word (Acts 6:1-7). Both apostles and deacons are servants. They only have different job descriptions.

Paul explained that he and Apollos, and I am sure he would include Peter and all the rest in this, are *"but ministers (diakonoi) by whom you believed"* (1 Cor. 3:5).

So, mother Mary tells the servants to do whatever Jesus says.

Obedience is the hallmark of the crucified ones. Anyone from this day onward who is not willing to lay down his own self-will in deference to the Head, Jesus Christ, and obey Him radically in every way, will miss out on this last and greatest miracle of God. Do whatever He says at all cost to yourself and your reputation!

Renewal of the Word

"And there were set there six waterpots of stone" (John 2:6). The number "six" in the Bible generally speaks of man.

I personally believe that 666 (Rev. 13:18) speaks of the fullness of man—that time when the carnal mind of man will have exalted itself to the maximum, above the knowledge of God. Although I do not disregard the possibility of an individual person to be the antichrist, the abomination that makes desolate the Holy Place (Matt. 24:15; Dan. 9:27), I am presently more concerned for the abomination of the carnal mind of Christians that is making desolate the Holy Place of their spirits.

The fact that there were six waterpots, I believe, speaks of this fullness of man, and that they were pots of stone speaks of our own lives as vessels. *"We have this treasure in earthen vessels..."* (2 Cor. 4:7).

It is therefore particularly significant that Jesus, who is Himself the Water of Life, should say to the servants (ministers), *"Fill the waterpots with water."* So *"they filled them up to the brim"* (John 2:7).

In the past two decades or so there has been a profound renewal in the word of God to the extent that many churches today rightly or wrongly call themselves "Word churches."

Among evangelicals, the emphasis has been upon correct interpretation of scriptural passages and deriving what is for them correct doctrines of the faith.

Among the charismatics, the emphasis has been upon knowing the word of God for yourself, confessing the word for the benefits it has promised, getting the word into your spirit and, among other things, using the word to defeat the powers of darkness.

This renewal in the word of God has shifted the emphasis away from the preeminence of church doctrines and dogmas to the point that many churchgoers have rejected the sanctity of their denominational doctrines altogether. To them it has become more than a matter of simply getting back to the Bible. It is a matter of getting hold of The Word.

But as I said in the beginning of this chapter, until the water of the word of God becomes the wine of the blood of God, it will have no redemptive value.

The servants obeyed! The preachers responded to this move of the Holy Spirit in the renewal of the word. They have filled the earthen vessels of word-hungry believers to the brim.

Now, the call goes out to these servants to draw some of the water out of the pots and take it to the one in charge of the feast. So far as we can tell at this point, the water is still water in the pots. But somewhere between the pot and the governor in charge, that water turned into wine.

Somewhere between the time that the obedient preacher preaches the anointed word of God and the time that it falls upon the ears of its doers, the water of the word must turn into the blood of the crucified life. Until it does, its redemptive power is null and void.

Renewal of the Blood

"When the ruler of the feast had tasted the water that was made wine, and knew not where it came from: (but the servants who drew the water knew;) the governor of the feast called the bridegroom, and said to him, 'Every man at the beginning sets forth good wine; and when men have well drunk, then that which is worse: but you have kept

the good wine until now.'" (John 2:9-10).

There has been a satisfaction of wine until now. Good wine. How can the wine of Jesus ever be anything but good and perfect? Yet, there is the promise of a better wine to come. The best shall come forth last; that is to say, the greatest move of the Holy Spirit is yet to come.

Just as there has been a renewal of the word during the past decades, there must now come a <u>renewal of the blood</u>. Not only will the revelation of the crucified life come forth, but that revelation will itself be coupled with the power of God to change the water into wine, the word into blood.

If the water of the word that anyone has is not allowed to be changed into the wine of His blood, that vessel will go into deception. There is a danger in acquiring knowledge for the sake of having knowledge or for the purposes of acquiring something for self.

You cannot have the word of God without the Lamb of God. *"This is He that came by water and blood, even Jesus Christ; not by water only, but by water and blood. And it is the Spirit that bears witness, because the Spirit is truth. For there are three that bear record in heaven, the Father, the Word, and the Holy Ghost: and these three are one. <u>And there are three that bear witness in earth, the Spirit, and the water, and the blood: and these three agree in one</u>"* (1 John 5:6-8).

First comes the water of the word, then the blood of the Lamb, and then the power of the Holy Spirit to transform the water of the word into the wine of the blood in all who take up their cross daily to follow Him. It takes all three to complete the witness of Christ in the earth whether in Christ Himself or in His crucified ones.

Yielding

No man can crucify himself. This is where the grace and power of God enters again and again. If any of us ever hope to be a part of this company, we must be willing to do the only thing possible for us to do: yield to the purging, purifying fire of the Holy Spirit whose desire it is to bring us into perfection. We can only <u>present ourselves</u> as a living sacrifice... (Rom. 12:1).

New Wine in New Wineskins

This new and better wine was offered at the wedding feast in Cana after all of the original wine had run out. The first was good as far as it went. But the portion we have had up until now is not sufficient to go the distance.

Permit me to change the analogy. The wine we've had up until now has been carried around in the wineskins of the traditions of men. These old wineskins have become hardened and brittle. They will not hold the new wine that is coming forth now. In many situations the gospel itself has been confused with the traditions of men that tried to contain it. The wineskins have been equated with the wine.

Flesh man always attempts to hold onto the moves of God by institutionalizing them. So they try to put them into skins of their own making. Sooner or later the emphasis is upon the glorification of the skin rather than the wine within. They become icons of our worship.

Every time we try to pour a new move of God into the old wineskins of our traditions, or when we try to freeze pack it so as to hold on to it forever, we promptly kill it.

God is not willing for His glory to be shared with flesh. He has not given us the Spirit to make the harlot church system look good.

This last, great, miraculous move of God whereby He changes the water into wine—the word into blood—cannot be poured into the old wineskins of churchianity. Don't look for the next, last, great revival to be inside the walls of denominations. It won't happen because it can't happen there. Those who expect to be a part of it are going to have to come out of them.

For this reason, He is devising for Himself His own wineskins for His miraculous new wine. It is the church without walls.

"This beginning of miracles Jesus did in Cana of Galilee, and manifested forth His glory; and His disciples believed in Him" (John 2:11).

The only way Jesus can be glorified is for Him to be lifted up in His crucified life. He said, *"And as Moses lifted up the serpent in the wilderness, even so must the Son of man be lifted up: that whosoever believes in Him should not perish, but have eternal life"* (John 3:14-15).

Again He said, *"'And I, if I am lifted up from the earth, will draw all men unto Me.' This He said, signifying what death He should die"* (John 12: 32-33).

Nothing has changed. The cross of Jesus Christ is still the only redemptive power in the world. And the only way Jesus is continually lifted up in such a way so as to draw all men unto Him is for all men to be able to see this crucified Jesus lived out in His crucified ones.

And insofar as those who follow Jesus in His baptism of sufferings, who follow the Lamb in radical obedience wherever He goes, being conformed into His image, allowing Him to be lived out in them as that many-membered, manifested man child—insofar as these become a reality, they are the new wine poured out in a new wineskin.

It is the very life of Jesus sacrificially being poured out again—this time through His crucified ones: the foretaste of Tabernacles.

Chapter 12

The Way, the Truth, and the Life

As recorded in John 14:2-6, Jesus comforted His disciples regarding His going away by telling them that if He goes, as He must, He will prepare a place for them in His Father's abode and will come again to receive them saying, *"that where I am, there you may be also."*

He continues, saying, *"And where I go you know, and the way you know."* But Thomas answered Him, *"Lord, we do not know where you go; and how can we know the way?"*

Jesus used the occasion to explain that He Himself is *"the way, and the truth, and the life."*

He is the Way, the Truth, and the Life, and it occurs in that order.

The Way

First, Jesus is the Way, the way unto salvation. No man can come to the Father except through Jesus (John 14:6b).

He clearly is the door of the sheep (John 10:7). Men try to enter the kingdom of God by many other ways. But they are thieves and robbers (John 10:1). No man can enter the Kingdom of God unless He is willing to humble himself in death and pass through the door who is the person of Jesus: to be buried with Him in His baptism and raised with Him in His resurrection (Rom 6:4).

This is the ministry of the outer court: the sacrifice of the Lamb of God, the Savior of the world. *"And you shall call His name Jesus: for He shall save his people from their sins"* (Matt. 1:21).

85

He is the way, the road, the narrow road that leads to life. *"Enter in at the strait gate: for wide is the gate, and broad is the way, that leads to destruction, and many there are who go in thereat: because strait is the gate, and narrow is the way, which leads to life, and few there are who find it"* (Matt. 7:13-14).

"There is a way that seems right to a man, but the end thereof are the ways of death" (Prov. 14:12).

That Jesus is the indisputable way of God unto God is the debate of carnal men to this day. It is an insult to the carnal mind of man which exalts itself above the knowledge of God that God should be so narrow minded. It insults the intellectual who wants either to believe that he has within himself the ability to save himself or, at best, that all religions funnel up to a common God.

But the revelation of God has come through the only begotten of God, Jesus, the Messiah of God. Jesus said, *"He who has seen Me has seen the Father"* (John 14:9). Now this is the way of God unto salvation. *"Whosoever shall call on the name of the Lord shall be saved"* (Acts 2:21). *"If you confess with your mouth the Lord Jesus, and shall believe in your heart that God raised Him from the dead, you shall be saved"* (Rom. 10:9).

The way is not a formula, a doctrine, a religion, or any such thing. The Way is the person of Jesus Christ. Jesus as the Way is the outer court of Passover.

The Truth

Jesus not only is first and foremost the Way, but He is the Truth. On numerous occasions He deliberately spoke to the Jews saying, *"I tell you the truth..."* (See John 8:40-46).

This He did not only to show the contrast between the truth and the hypocrisy of the religion of the Pharisees, but to declare who He Himself was.

He didn't just tell the truth. He didn't merely know the truth. He was the Truth.

Jesus told the Jews who believed in Him to abide in His word. He didn't say abide in His words, but in His word (John 8:31NAS). This was just another way of His saying "*abide in Me*" as He illustrated in John 15:1-8 (which speaks of the true vine and the branches) . For Jesus was the Word of God made flesh.

"*In the beginning was the Word, and the Word was with God, and the Word was God... And the Word was made flesh and dwelt among us...*" (John 1:1,14).

If you who believe abide in His word, that is, abide in Him, then three things are promised: (1) you are indeed His disciple, (2) you shall know the truth, and (3) the truth shall make you free (John 8:31-32).

The Jews boasted to Jesus that they were descendants of Abraham and had never been in bondage to anyone (John 8:33). How could He have the audacity to say He could set them free?

Jesus explained that they were enslaved to sin (v.34). This was particularly hard for them to believe, being Jews who rigidly kept the Law and had made many laws of their own. Yet, Jesus accused them of being in bondage to sin.

They had yet to understand that "*the letter [law] kills, but the Spirit gives life*" (2 Cor. 3:6).

So we move from Jesus, the Savior, to Jesus, the Truth. Jesus is the truth and He promised to send the Holy Spirit of truth.

Jesus instructed His disciples saying, "*But when the Comforter is come, whom I will send to you from the Father, even the Spirit of truth, which proceeds from the Father, He will testify of Me*" (John 15:26).

Later He said, "*When He, the Spirit of truth is come, He will guide you into all truth; for He shall not speak of Himself; but whatever He shall hear, that shall He speak...*" (John 16:13).

Jesus, the Way, is clearly pointing beyond Passover to Jesus, the Truth, in the person of the Holy Spirit who is the promise of the Father: The Spirit of truth.

"*But the anointing which you have received of Him abides in you, and you need not that any man teach you: but as the same anointing teaches you of all things, and is truth, and is no lie, and even as it has taught you, you shall abide in Him*" (1 John 2:27).

While Jesus and His Spirit are inseparable, He, nevertheless, explains Himself in these various manifestations: first He is the Way, then He is the Truth. The only way we can know the truth is to have the Holy Spirit reveal it to us. Thus we move from the outer court of Passover to the Holy Place of Pentecost.

The Life

But the Spirit of truth is always going to point back to Jesus.

"He [the Spirit] shall glorify Me: for He shall receive of Mine, and shall show it to you" (John 16:14).

The Spirit of truth is always going to bring us back to Jesus, the Savior—back to the cross. But the irony is this: that the pointing back to Jesus is always a going on in Him, a pressing onward and upward. It is a going on from Passover to Pentecost to Tabernacles, even the tabernacle of David. For the tabernacle of David is that which is promised for the end, not the tabernacle of Moses.

"After this I will return, and will build again the tabernacle of David, which is fallen down; and I will build again the ruins thereof, and I will set it up" (Acts 15:16,17).

The tabernacle of Moses had the Holy of Holies behind the great veil in which was the ark of the covenant, the mercy seat on top of the ark, and the cherubim resting at the ends of the mercy seat (Ex. 25). Only the high priest was permitted to enter the Holy of Holies, once a year, to atone for his sins first and for all the sins of the people (Lev. 16, Heb. 9:2-7).

By contrast, the tabernacle of David was merely a tent stretched out on Mount Zion and the only article in it was the ark of the covenant (1 Chron. 16:1).

The ark of the covenant was made of acacia wood overlaid with gold and originally had within it the tablets of stone upon which was written the ten commandments, the jar with manna, and the budding rod of Aaron (Heb. 9:4).

The ark itself speaks of Jesus Christ. The acacia wood represented His humanity, and the gold overlay represented His deity.

The tablets with the Ten Commandments represented the Word of God. Jesus is the Word. So in this, the tablets of stone represented Jesus.

The manna was likened unto Jesus who is that living bread of life that comes down out of heaven (John 6:49-51).

The budding rod of Aaron (Num. 17) represented the authority of the Lord Jesus Christ as the great High Priest who entered the Holy of Holies once for all to atone for the sins of the world. *"We have such a high priest, who is set on the right hand of the throne of the Majesty on the heavens; a minister of the sanctuary, and of the true tabernacle, which the Lord pitched, and not man"* (Heb. 8:1-2).

This leads us to say that when it comes to the tabernacle of David, Jesus is all in all.

There is coming that time when the Spirit of truth will bring us to that resting place in Jesus where, by revelation, we grasp the reality that Jesus has finished the works of God, that He is all in all, that He is the only thing there is.

Once the true believer grasps hold of this reality, it will set him free. *"If the Son therefore shall make you free, you shall be free indeed"* (John 8:36).

So, He who is the Way leads to the Truth; and He who is the Truth leads onward, upward to the Life.

Having arrived at Bethany to raise Lazarus from the dead (John 11:17-40), Jesus said of Himself to Martha, *"I am the resurrection and the life. He who believes in Me, though he was dead, yet shall he live."*

Mary ran out to where Jesus was. Weeping, she said, *"Lord, if you had been here, my brother would not have died."*

Jesus groaned in His spirit and later wept. They thought He wept over Lazarus because of His love for him. But I believe He wept over their lack of perception—not just their unbelief, but over their failure to recognize Him as the life-giver from God.

Jesus said to Martha, *"Did I not say to you, that, if you would believe, you should see the glory of God?"*

The life-giver, Jesus, has now put all of this in the reference of glory. Thus, we have moved from <u>Jesus, the Way</u>, the outer court of Passover, that which redeems and justifies, to <u>Jesus, the Truth</u>, the Holy Place of Pentecost, that which sanctifies (separates) and empowers us, onward to

Jesus the Life, the Holy of Holies of Tabernacles, that which glorifies both the Father and His sons.

Therefore, let us go into Him who has gone before us into the Holy of Holies, that we might truly abide in Him and He abide in us.

Chapter 13

God's Finished Work

Sometimes we have to break a thing down and look at its parts before we can see and appreciate it as a whole. That is what this study into the three courts and feasts has intended in part to do.

All of these mighty acts of God (justification, sanctification, glorification; that is, salvation) were accomplished by Jesus in His finished work upon the cross. When He died, the Bible says that the veil of the Temple was torn in two (Matt. 27:51). This indicates to us that we now have access to the Father through the death of Jesus Christ because He entered once and for all into the Holy of Holies as the great High Priest (Heb. 9:11-12; 10:19-22).

The only way that any of us have access to the Father is through Jesus Christ who is *"the way and the truth and the life"* (John 14:6). And because of what He did then, we are now seated with Him in the heavenlies (Eph. 2:6). We can come boldly into the throne room before God (Heb. 4.10).

It is not as though we have to qualify on the basis of works to pass through one degree to another until we come to that third degree. That's the way it is with secret orders.

God intended from the beginning that every believer should come fully into a place where Jesus Christ is absolute Lord. It should never happen that one is first converted and "saved," receiving, as it is preached, "Jesus into his heart as Savior," then weeks, months, years later have to be convinced that he must further make Him Lord. Jesus is not Savior until He is Lord. Only when He is Lord are we properly related to Him. Only when He is Lord is He permitted by our God-given free wills to work out His salvation in us. *"If you shall confess with your mouth the Lord Jesus, and shall believe in your heart that God has raised Him from the dead, you shall be saved."* (Rom. 10:9). The New American Standard says *"...if you confess with your mouth Jesus as Lord."* Lordship is the prerequisite to salvation.

The Full, Full Gospel

The more we read the Bible, the more we discover the "is-ness" of God, that God "is" and that all things in Him are accomplished facts, that all one needs to do is to believe.

Again I say, Ephesians 2:8 is the plumb line. *"For by grace are you saved through faith..."* Grace is God's part. Faith is our part. God's already done His part. It is finished. All we have to do in order to make it applicable in our lives is to believe—not passive mental assent to God and to Jesus Christ as the Son of God, but active faith that comes by revelation knowledge and quickens new life to our spirits.

Christ is our justification, our righteousness, our redemption, our sanctification, our glorification, our salvation. He is our all in all. It is all in who He is. So that when we come to Him in radical belief, surrender, and total abandonment, we have obtained all of who He is. One should be able to go from justification to glorification in one swift conversion experience.

So why doesn't it happen that way? I suggest two reasons: one is because Tabernacles, although fulfilled in Jesus, has itself not yet been fulfilled in terms of God's own historical timetable. There have been many great saints throughout the ages who have lived such a crucified life, but the promise of glorification is reserved for the end. *"Beloved, now we are the sons of God, and it does not yet appear what we shall be: but we know that, when He shall appear, we shall be like Him; for we shall see Him as He is"* (1 John 3:2).

The other reason we have not gone from justification to glorification in one conversion experience is simply because it has not been preached that way. *"Faith comes by hearing and hearing by the word of God"* (Rom. 10:17). Whatever is preached is generally believed and received.

We have not preached the full gospel yet. The evangelicals preach repentance and the new birth, so people repent and are born again. The Pentecostals and charismatics came along with the revelation of the baptism in the Holy Spirit, speaking in unknown tongues, healing miracles, and claim to be preaching the full gospel. To the extent those truths are preached can they be believed, received, and actualized. But to preach only Passover, or Passover and Pentecost is not yet the full gospel. Only two of the three feasts are preached.

If the evangelists were to preach the Lordship of Jesus Christ and the laid-down life, if people fully understood the cost of discipleship and decided to follow Jesus anyway, they would be sold out from the beginning and would not have to be dragged from one court to the other.

Once a false teaching has been received, it is hard to part with. If we have been taught that the baptism in the Holy Spirit and tongues are not for today, it is hard to pull down those strongholds in the mind. If one is taught a deceptive version of faith and prosperity, it is hard to move him on into the deeper things of God. Whatever is preached is most likely going to be that which is believed.

But in this last day, before the Lord comes, He is purifying the message of the gospel. He is restoring the good news of *"Jesus Christ and Him crucified"* (1 Cor. 2:2).

The gospel truth is that we are called not to be saved from hell so we can go to heaven when we die. That's a by-product of our salvation. We have not been saved so we can attain all the creature comforts for the flesh in this life. We have been called to follow Jesus in His baptism which is the only way to glorify Father.

Just as the Son sought only to glorify Father, so are His many sons to seek only to glorify Him. That is our sole purpose for living as sons of God.

And just as the Son was glorified when He sought only to glorify the Father, so will the many sons be glorified only as they seek to glorify the Father.

The only way the Son glorified the Father was through radical obedience. Thus, it shall also be with the many sons.

If we are willing to sell out completely to Him up front, we can come into that fullness in Him. Or we can take the forty year journey in the wilderness in order to get there. But the latter is the harder road to travel. Those who rebelled in the wilderness died in the wilderness. They failed to enter into the promises of God.

The flesh never wants to sell out to the Spirit. It is sold out to itself. The spirit man walks according to the Spirit of God and not according to the flesh (Gal. 5:16).

"For whosoever shall call upon the name of the Lord Jesus Christ shall be saved" (Rom. 10:13). We are to call upon Lord ... Jesus ... Christ; that is, King ... Savior ... Anointer. When He becomes Lord to you by revelation, He becomes your Savior. When He is Savior, He is the Anointer. *"...He shall baptize you with the Holy Ghost and with fire"* (Matt. 3:11).

Pressing on Toward the Mark

In setting forth the gospel message in terms of these three courts and feasts, we actually see that they represent a progression in history of the fulfillment of God's plan in the world, that Jesus Christ as Lord is the fulfillment of them in the fullness of time, that they represent three stages believers themselves can enter into, and that one does not have to linger in either of the former courts but can and must go on to fullness in God.

I desire for you to learn these differences, but I desire more that this study in God's word will catapult everyone of you to that place with Paul, the apostle, who could say of himself,

"But what things were gain to me, those I counted loss for Christ. Yes doubtless, and I count all things but loss for the excellency of the knowledge of Christ Jesus my Lord: for whom I have suffered the loss of all things, and do count them but dung, that I may win Christ, and be found in Him, not having my own righteousness, which is of the Law, but that which is through the faith of Christ, the

righteousness which is of God by faith: <u>that I may know Him, and the power of his resurrection, and the fellowship of His sufferings, being made conformable unto His death;</u> if by any means I might attain unto the resurrection of the dead. Not as though I had already attained, either were already perfect: but I follow after, if that I may apprehend that for which also I am apprehended of Christ Jesus. Brethren, I count not myself to have apprehended: but this one thing I do, forgetting those things which are behind, and reaching forth into those things which are before, I <u>press toward the mark for the prize of the high calling of God in Christ Jesus</u>" (Phil. 3:7-14).

Chapter 14

Inheriting the Kingdom of Heaven

Entering the Kingdom of heaven is the act of entering into a whole new realm of reality. You see things about God, yourself, and life that you've never seen before, you know things that you've never known before, and you understand things that you've never understood before.

To begin with, you come to a realization of the kingship of Jesus Christ. If you ever doubted it before, standing in the Kingdom and seeing Him by way of spiritual eyes removes all doubt. This is truth that comes by way of revelation knowledge.

When the Father opens your eyes to see this new realm of reality, you have faith to believe in the lordship of Jesus Christ. That is, you have faith to trust in Him as Lord of all of your life. Until you know that you know that Jesus is Lord of all, you have not fully come into the Kingdom of heaven.

According to New Testament scripture, we can see the Kingdom, we can enter the Kingdom, and we can inherit the Kingdom. People who stand in the outer court of Passover at best can only see the Kingdom. They do not enjoy the privileges of entering into it and inheriting it.

Those who go from Passover to Pentecost not only see the Kingdom but enter into it. The mere act of entering the Kingdom changes one's perspective on reality. Suddenly, one is able to discern spiritual matters. The scriptures come alive, and one begins to move in the gifts of the Spirit and begins to bear more of the fruit of the Spirit.

Those who hunger and thirst for a hundredfold life in Christ not only enter but begin to inherit the Kingdom. We have been made heirs and joint-heirs with Christ. That is to say, all of who He is, what He is, and what He possesses as the Lord of glory in His Kingdom is equally ours.

This makes absolutely no sense to the carnal mind of unredeemed man who has neither seen nor entered the Kingdom. When the people of Passover begin to talk about their salvation, the people of the world cringe with disbelief. They have no basis for believing in what they cannot see.

Not everyone who has seen the Kingdom has entered it. Not everyone who has entered the Kingdom has inherited.

No one has, as yet in this life, completely inherited the Kingdom. We inherit the Kingdom by degrees. We take the land little by little. Once we, by the Spirit, have conquered one area of Kingdom living whereby we can live in complete assurance by faith, then we can go on to the next plane of reality. That which is of the Spirit is more real than those things of the natural world. *"While we look not at the things which are seen, but at the things which are not seen: for the things which are seen are temporal; but the things which are not seen are eternal"* (2 Cor. 4:18).

Every time we see a new thing by the Spirit about the Kingdom, we inherit that, we come into that, we have the courage of faith to walk in that; then, that becomes a manifested reality in our lives.

Only the people of Tabernacles can inherit the Kingdom in fullness because it calls for the total surrender of all. This is not intended to suggest elitism. On the contrary, the cost to the crucified ones is great. They have to sacrifice fame, fortune, prestige, recognition, traditional ministry, power, position, and reputation. They are misunderstood and often accounted as heretics.

Nevertheless, the rewards of the Kingdom make it all worth the cost. For the people of Tabernacles and of the Holy of Holies come to a place in Jesus where nothing else matters—and that is the ultimate inheritance.

Chapter 15

Standing in the Gap

Ezekiel 22:30 reads, *"And I sought for a man among them, that should make up the hedge, and stand in the gap before Me for the land, that I should not destroy it: but I found none."*

This word came to me in 1983:

"I am looking for a man," says the Lord, "who will stand in the gap for Me. One who will battle the enemy on behalf of the Church. One who will dare to put on the full armor of God, the full battle array, and be all that I require of him to be.

"I require much of this man. More than he could ever hope to be in and of himself.

"I require him to be holy.

"I require of him to be pure in heart.

"I require him to be loving and humble and gentle and wise and strong.

"I require him to be knowledgeable of My word and perfectly obedient to it.

"I require of him the high praises of God.

"I require of him prayer, the kind that ascends to My throne room where I can answer in power and might.

"I require of him perfect obedience to all that I say for him to do: to go where I say go, to do what I say do, and be what I say be.

"I require of him faith, the kind that moves mountains.

"I require of him to lay down his life for others, to prefer others above himself, to give no thought for tomorrow or for his life.

"I require of him to be different, peculiar, elusive, misunderstood, despised by many, hated, persecuted, abused; and amidst it all I require that he turn the other cheek.

"I require of him mercy.

"I require of him power to cast out demons, to heal the sick, to set the captives free, to proclaim the acceptable year of the Lord.

"I require of him to be perfectly conformed to the image of My Son, whose name is above every name in heaven, on earth, and beneath the earth.

"I require him to be just like Jesus.

"I not only require all of this from him, but I will also give him the ability to meet these requirements. I give him Jesus.

"If he will only turn to Me with a whole heart, abandon everything else in his heart, make Jesus Lord of his life, I will deposit the very life of Jesus in his heart through My Holy Spirit; and then I will have found the man I've been looking for. And he will stand in the gap for me."

Chapter 16

The Bride

There is only one story from the beginning to the end in the Bible.

It is a story of love between a husband and His intended wife.

The story begins with a wedding, the wedding of two people, man and woman. *"...and they shall be one flesh"* (Gen. 2:24).

This first man (Adam) was made after the image of God and was planned of God to be as a son to Him.

This first man, however, fell from fellowship with his Father-Creator when He disobeyed Him in the garden of life. Having fallen, he was driven from that garden to live under the curse of death. Death is the absence of life. God is life and Adam was no longer in the presence of Life. *"For the wages of sin is death"* (Rom. 6:23).

With this story begins a love affair between the Creator and His created one.

God and Israel

Throughout the Bible, God was viewed as a husband and Israel, His chosen one, was viewed as His bride.

The most striking example of this is recorded in Jeremiah 3:6-8. It was after Israel was divided between the northern Kingdom of Israel and the southern Kingdom of Judah. The Lord spoke to Jeremiah in the days when Josiah was King saying, *"Have you seen that which backsliding Israel has done? She has gone up upon every high mountain and under every green tree, and there has played the harlot.*

"And I said after she had done all these things, 'Turn unto Me.' But she did not return. And her treacherous sister Judah saw it.

"And I saw, when for all the causes whereby backsliding Israel committed adultery I had put her away, and given her a bill of divorce; yet her treacherous sister Judah did not fear, but went and played the harlot also."

God had chosen Israel through Abraham, Isaac, and Jacob to be to Him a people of His own choosing. *"For you are a holy people to the Lord your God, and the Lord has chosen you to be a peculiar people unto Himself, above all the nations that are upon the earth"* (Deut. 14: 2).

But because of her idolatry—going after other gods, the foremost thing God warned against—God called Israel and Judah a harlot. This is most vividly described in Ezekiel 16. Read it!

Hosea, the prophet, depicts this husband and wife relationship between God and Israel in terms of his own life. He is called upon by God to marry a harlot. Yet, even after she leaves him to return to her harlotry, he shows forth his great love for her by purchasing her off of the auction block.

In this great story God is seen as wooing harlot Israel back by his love. She is unwilling to love Him, seemingly incapable of doing so, so He purchases her Himself. Of course, we see this now in view of the act of God's redemption in Christ Jesus our Lord who shed His precious blood to purchase us from sin and deliver us from idolatry.

God and the Church

This husband and wife relationship carries over into the New Testament with Jesus as the husband and the church as the bride.

It is impossible to see Israel and the church as separate entities. The church of Jesus Christ is merely the extension of Israel as God's chosen people. Israel and the church are one personality throughout history.

Whatever was Israel's history is our history in the church today. Abraham is every bit our Father. His history is our history. When we read of Isaac and Jacob, we are reading about our spiritual ancestors. We identify with them and they with us as being a part of that one body, one man, one person, one bride.

But the church today, just as it was true of Israel then, is just as capable of idolatry. We are just as likely to play the harlot as she.

Jesus and His Bride

John the Baptist recognized this relationship between Jesus and the church as a bride when he announced that *"He who has the bride is the bridegroom"* (John 3:29).

Paul wrote the Corinthians saying, *"For I am jealous over you with godly jealousy: for I have espoused you to one husband, that I may present you as a chaste virgin to Christ"* (2 Cor. 11:2).

Paul wrote to the church at Ephesus and compared the relationship between Jesus and the church with that of a husband and wife. In this beautiful passage, Paul is saying in so many words that the husband is to show forth the likeness of Christ to the wife and the wife is to show forth the likeness of the church to the husband; that is, the husband is a type of Christ in the home and the wife is a type of the church (Eph. 5:21-33).

The word for church in the Greek is *ekklesia* which actually means "called-out-ones" and is feminine in gender.

In this passage from Ephesians 5, we read, *"Husbands love your wives, even as Christ also loved the church and gave Himself for it; that He might sanctify and cleanse it with the washing of water by the word, that He might present it to Himself a glorious church, not having spot, or wrinkle; but that it should be holy and without blemish."*

The Greek word from which the pronoun "it" is translated is *autes* which means, "he," "she," or "it" depending upon the gender of its antecedent. In this case the antecedent of *autes* is *ekklesia;* therefore, "it" should be translated "her." It is unfortunate that the translators mistakenly used "church" instead of "called-out ones" and "it" instead of "her" because this emphasizes that false notion that the church is a thing instead of a person.

One of the greatest idolatries that has crept upon the

body of Christ throughout the Christian era is this eleva-
tion of institutional Christianity. In many, many cases
one's church, as an institution, has become a greater love
than one's obedience to Christ. All that pertains to institutional Christianity is assumed to be the gospel.

We love our church. We serve our church. We join our
church. We try to get others to join it. We compete with
other churches over who is the best, who is the biggest, and
who is right. Our churches have become our "high places"
wherein we worship ourselves, pretending to be worship-
ing God.

There is a legitimate scriptural mandate for us not to
forsake the assembling of ourselves together. *"And let us
consider one another to provoke to love and to good
works: not forsaking the assembling of ourselves together,
as is the manner of some; but exhorting one another: and
so much the more, as you see the day approaching"* (Heb.
10:24-25). There is a big difference between assembling for
the sake of perpetuating the local church or the denomina-
tion of which we may be a part and assembling to provoke
one another to love and to good works.

We not only are to come together as the body of Christ,
but we are to be assembled by the leadership of the Holy
Spirit. It is one thing to go to "church" and quite another
to be assembled as the church (called-out-ones for assembly into Christ).

The Spotless Bride

We are the body of Christ, and as His body we are His
bride in waiting. And, just as it has always been, God is
still wooing us to love Him and Him only. He is still court-
ing us that He might be our first love.

It is one thing to say we love God, but the real test of our
love is in our obedience. Jesus said in John 14:15, *"If you
love Me, keep My commandments."* (The New American
Standard translation says, *"If you love Me, you will keep
My commandments.)*

Jesus is coming for His bride.

He is coming for a bride without spot or wrinkle (Eph.
5:27).

He Himself was the Lamb of God without blemish and without spot (1 Pet. 1:19). That unblemished Lamb can only be joined as one flesh to an unblemished bride. That is why we can only be redeemed with His precious blood and not with corruptible things. (1 Pet. 1:18).

The bride without spot or wrinkle is she who has kept the faith; that is, has been faithful to her first and only love, Jesus Christ, her Lord. She is a true lover.

A Loving Bride

Jesus said, *"If you keep My commandments, you shall abide in My love; even as I have kept My Father's commandments, and abide in His love.... This is My commandment, that you love one another, as I have loved you"* (John 15:10,12).

There will be more judgment against the church for not having loved one another than perhaps any other thing. It is first, foremost, and probably the most difficult of all things to do. But God considers the love of the brethren as being equal with our love for Him.

It is vitally important that we keep His commandment because, as Jesus said, *"By this shall all men know that you are My disciples, if you have love one to another"* (John 13:35).

We say we want to be witnesses for Him, and by that we often mean we want to win somebody to the Lord. Yet, the greatest witness is going to be on the basis of our love one to another.

How do we love one another? Jesus showed us how in His own laid-down life. *"Greater love has no man than this, that a man lay down his life for his friends"* (John 15:13). Jesus called those who do what He says, His friends (John 15:14). If, as obedient ones, we are regarded as His friends, we best consider one another friends in this same way—laying down our lives in love for each other. It helps me to say it this way: lay down self for one another.

There is no way we can come into the deeper things of God, no way we can approach the great throne room of God, no way we can enter into that Holy of Holies without loving as He loved.

To be faithful to Jesus is to be faithful to one another. To love Him is to love one another. For we are all His body. Whatever we say or do against one another we have done it unto Him.

When Saul of Tarsus was persecuting the followers of Jesus, the Lord Jesus confronted him on the road to Damascus one day, appearing in a blinding light, and asked him, *"Saul, Saul, why do you persecute Me?"* (Acts 9:4). Jesus had already ascended into heaven and was seated at the right hand of the Father. How could Saul persecute Jesus? Simply by persecuting His followers. Has anything changed today?

A Holy Bride

To traverse from the outer court of Passover onward to the Holy Place of Pentecost and the Holy of Holies of Tabernacles is to go from faith to faith, glory to glory; that is, to go on to greater love and faithfulness: holiness.

To go on to greater love and faithfulness is to be separated from all that is displeasing to God. It is a walk of true holiness.

Many interpret holiness, whether consciously or not, as ascribing to a system of moral codes intended to control the outward behavior of its believers and ascribing to certain doctrines as law.

But true holiness is summed up into one basic commandment: love. If you love God with all of your heart, soul, mind, and strength, everything else will fall into place. You will separate yourself from sin and idolatry. You will love your neighbor as yourself. You will involve yourself in the family of God, encouraging and strengthening one another in the household of God. You will see to it that there is plenty of oil in your lamp.

An abundance of Christians today are anxiously awaiting the rapture of the church. Their eyes are more on the rapture and their hearts are more intent upon escape than upon the Lord. The true bride, on the contrary, is anxiously awaiting that glorious day when she will be joined with her love. But she does not want that day to come before she has made herself ready.

That day is rapidly coming, but it will not come until the bride has made herself ready.

"'Let us be glad and rejoice, and give honor to Him: for the marriage of the Lamb is come, and His wife has made herself ready.' And to her was granted that she should be arrayed in fine linen, clean and white: for the fine linen is the righteousness of saints. And He said to me, 'Write, Blessed are they who are called to the marriage supper of the Lamb'" (Rev. 19:7-9).

The love affair between God and His people carries on to this day. And in this day, God is separating the wheat from the chaff, the bride from the harlot. He is exposing the harlot and revealing the bride.

As we see more and more of what the nature of the bride is, that revelation will itself and on its own call the bride forth.

A Remnant Bride

It is important now for all true believers to take seriously that mandate of Christ to *"look up, lift up your heads, for your redemption draws near"* (Luke 21:28).

Our redemption has always depended and continues to depend wholly and totally upon Christ and His shed blood as the Lamb of God. He has chosen us. We are called of Him.

Nevertheless, He Himself said, *"Many are called, but few are chosen"* (Matt. 22:14).

Throughout Israel's history God always promised Himself that a remnant would be saved. God has always dealt with remnants. There is going to be a remnant church. There is going to be a people called out of a people in this last day who will show forth the glory of the Lord, who will emerge as the bride without spot or wrinkle, who are faithful and loving.

This remnant will not consist of all who merely claim to be Christian, though many of them will be saved. It will not include even the many well meaning Christians who are jumping for joy over the prospects of the rapture. It will include only those who are committed to faithfully following the Lamb wherever He goes. *"These are they which were not defiled with women; for they are virgins.*

107

These are they who follow the Lamb wherever He goes"
(Rev. 14:4).

This is not an elite group of people as the world would measure it. They are hidden, faceless, a people who bear the image of their Father, who walk not after the flesh but after the Spirit, who bear fruit a hundredfold, who dare to die to self that His life might be lived out through them, who enter into the Holy of Holies where Jesus is the only thing there is, who are purged, purified by the sanctifying work of the Holy Spirit and are well on their way to being glorified—not in the exaltation of self, but in the total denial of self.

Someone asked me once, "Who are the ten virgins spoken of in Matthew 25:1-13?"

I had always assumed they were the bride. But the question caused me to realize that they could not have been the bride, at least not all ten of them, since the five foolish virgins were not allowed in. The bride is not divided that way.

It came to me later on in the context of this study that the five who did not have sufficient oil represented those thirtyfold believers who were content to camp out in the outer court of Passover and refused to get for themselves the oil of the Holy Spirit. They had their lamps which had been lit by the oil of the Spirit, but they needed more if they were to go the distance into the midnight.

I know this offends our orthodoxy, but consider what John said in Revelation 11:1-2. *"And there was given to me a reed like a rod: and the angel stood, saying, 'Rise, and measure the temple of God, and the altar, and them that worship therein. But the court which is without the temple leave out, and measure it not; for it is given to the Gentiles: and the holy city shall they tread under foot forty-two months.'"*

The other five virgins had enough oil and were able to attend the wedding feast. These are those sixtyfold believers whom I suggest have willingly received the baptism in the Holy Spirit, who went beyond the outer court of Passover to the Holy Place of Pentecost, but who stopped there. They began to gather around the gifts instead of the

Giver and in many subtle ways tended to exalt themselves in pride rather than allowing that anointing to bring them to the end of themselves.

They are able to attend the wedding, but they are not the bride. They have played the harlot, for spiritual harlotry is anything for self. But just as Israel was not God's people because He had divorced them, there remained the promise that they would once again be His people (Hos. 1:9-10). So it is with the adulterous church. God will redeem.

I suggest that the bride without spot or wrinkle was already at the wedding feast with the Bridegroom when the call went out. *"He who has the bride is the bridegroom."* These are hundredfold believers.

The heart of God goes out today in advance of the great and terrible day of the Lord and is calling forth the bride. He who has ears let him hear.

Chapter 17

Zion

Israel/Judah/Zion

In Old Testament times Israel was divided into two kingdoms: the northern kingdom of Israel, sometimes called by the name of its major city, Samaria; and the southern kingdom of Judah, which included the city of Jerusalem.

The northern kingdom, Israel, was given by God the name Aholah (Ezek. 23:4ff). She played the harlot to the point that God sent her into oblivion, never to be restored—only a remnant was to return. Aholah means "(she has) her own tent." This name might have to do with the fact that Israel under Jeroboam abandoned the worship of Yahweh in Jerusalem and established his own center of idol worship in Samaria (1 Kings 12:25-33).

The southern kingdom of Judah was called her sister and named Aholibah (Ezek. 23:4ff) which means "my tent is in her." This name might have been given to Judah to signify that the Temple was in Jerusalem as the true center of worship of Yahweh. In spite of this fact and in spite of having seen what her treacherous sister did and what happened to her, Judah committed the same atrocities against God. So she was exiled to Babylon for seventy years (Jer. 25:11).

But the call of God went forth to the captives in Babylon: *"My people, go out of the midst of her..."* (Jer. 51:45). We are to return to Zion, the holy mountain of God (Jer. 31:6). Zion is that place where the tabernacle of David rested, where Jesus is the only thing there is.

Northern Israel is likened unto those who are in the

outer court, institutional Christianity, those who are full of idolatry, those who are not to be included when the measuring rod of God is put to the church.

Southern Judah is likened unto the Pentecostals and charismatics who once saw the atrocities of their older sister, and came out of her to be led by the Spirit to higher ground.

Soon, however, she became just as institutional, just as self-centered, just as legalistic, just as idolatrous as her sister. The only difference perhaps is that she took with her, in addition to her lamp, a vessel of oil—the oil of the Holy Spirit. She made it in as an attendant to the bride but is not the bride (Matt. 25:1-13).

That's as far as she goes. The cry to go on to Zion is not in her heart. Only a remnant returned from Babylon with Zerubbabel, Ezra, and Nehemiah. Most of the rest were content to stay in the comfort of their Babylonian cities.

The way was not easy for those who came out of Babylon to return to Jerusalem. They had to constantly contend with the taunting, threatening enemy in the land.

Repairing the Wall

Those who returned had two major tasks on their hands. One was to rebuild the wall around Jerusalem. This is a type of the spiritual warfare that is being accomplished through the prayer warriors whom God is raising up today. Thank God for that army of faceless intercessors who are doing battle for the rest of the camp.

There have been many breaches in the wall around the church, many places where the enemy has been able to enter and ravage the city of God. They are breaches of disdain for one another, mean legalism, dogmatism, and sectarianism.

Those breaches are being repaired. Just as it was in the days of Ezra and Nehemiah, so is it today. Every man must repair the wall where he lives. He is to hold his tool in one hand and his weapon in another. I think *agape* (self-sacrificing love) is the tool and prayer is the weapon.

Nothing is going to be accomplished for God in this hour unless it is first accomplished in prayer.

Rebuilding the Temple

The other task at hand was to rebuild the temple that had been destroyed.

This is exactly what God is doing today. He is bringing his body together. There is only *"one body, and one Spirit...one Lord, one faith, one baptism, one God and Father of all, who is above all, and through all, and in you all"* (Eph. 4:4-6).

This is not being accomplished in the ecumenical movement of institutional Christianity. It is accomplished only by this remnant who is willing to answer the call of God to *"come out of her, My people"* (Rev. 18:4). *"Come, and let us go up to the mountain of the Lord, to the house of the God of Jacob; and He will teach us of His ways, and we will walk in His paths..."* (Is. 2:3).

This remnant is the church without walls. The coming together of the fivefold ministry to truly equip the saints for the work of service—a people who gather only in the name of Jesus for strength and who go out in the power of the Spirit for service.

The only wall around them is that wall of fire spoken of in Zechariah 2:5: *"'For I,' says the Lord, 'will be unto her a wall of fire round about, and will be the glory in the midst of her.'"*

Returning to Zion

So, the bride is not the northern kingdom of Israel, institutional Christianity, nor the southern kingdom left in Babylon, but those straggly few who dare to take up the cause of God to return to Zion.

They are the Zion of God.

It is from them that the word goes forth. *"...For out of Zion shall go forth the law, and the word of the Lord from Jerusalem [the remnant]"* (Is. 2:3).

Restoring the Prophetic Ministry

Were it not for the prophets of God in Zerubbabel's day who encouraged them to keep on building and not be discouraged by the enemy, they may never have finished their tasks (Ezra 5:1-2; 6:14).

There is a restoration of the prophetic ministry today. While many prophets are handing out encouragements with personal prophecies, and many others are accurately predicting situations, the true prophet is also going to be speaking the words from God that call His people to repent, to come out of Babylon, to come to Zion, to holiness. He will call forth the bride.

The prophetic ministry today is likened unto John the Baptist as one crying in the wilderness, *"Prepare ye the way of the Lord"* (Matt. 3:3).

The coming forth of the bride, the preparation of the bride for His coming is the preparation of the way of the Lord.

For God is coming for His bride. That's what the whole story of the Bible is about. If we lose sight of that, we miss the whole point of scripture and of the purposes of God.

It is best that we devote our time and energies not so much in trying to attain things from God, or in getting our doctrines in agreement with one another, or in building large congregations and bigger buildings, but in seeking the face of our Bridegroom.

She has made herself ready. Ah, that's the key. Yet, not I, but Christ who lives in me.

As It Was in the Beginning

Now observe this final principle: as it was in the beginning so shall it be in the end.

The first Adam was made at the hands of God. From his side came forth his bride. Thus:

Out of the man came the woman.

Jesus was born of the virgin Mary. She was conceived by the Most High God when the Holy Spirit came upon her (Luke 1:35).

Mary is a type of the mother-church. The Holy Spirit brought forth a spiritual Son, the only begotten of the Father. Mary was chosen because she found favor with God (Luke 1:30). Thus:

Out of the woman came a man.

Then Jesus died on the cross and shed His precious blood. From His side flowed both the water and the blood and in so doing He gave birth to the church. Thus:

Out of the man came a woman.

Now in this last hour, God intends to repeat the cycle as the mother-church, according to Revelation 12, travails in childbirth to bring forth the man child.

Jesus was the Son of God. Now God is revealing many sons brought to glory. Thus:

Out of the woman came a man child.

Then, in the final cycle, this man child will give birth to that prepared bride who is without spot or wrinkle or any such thing. Thus:

Out of the man came a woman, the bride.

Out of the man came the woman: Eve
Out of the woman came the man: Jesus
Out of the man came the woman: Church
Out of the woman came the man: Man child—a many-membered son.

Out of the man came the woman: The bride.

As it was in the beginning so shall it be in the end.

From Passover to Pentecost to Tabernacles (Zion).

When, in the sight of God, a man is joined to his wife, they two become one flesh. The bride of Christ is one with Christ, made ready before He comes. She becomes Him, abiding in Him and He in her.

When God reproduces children, He reproduces children after His own kind—seed of His seed.

The mother, therefore, being one with God, is bringing forth children of the God-kind. So, God is coming for Himself. He will catch up unto Himself and unto His throne those who bear His image, who are seed of His seed, sons of God: His crucified ones.

He who has ears to hear, let him hear.